Fog Island

Fog Island

A
Vancouver Island
Circumnavigation
Full of Surprises

Norm Culver

SEAWORTHY PUBLICATIONS, INC. • MELBOURNE, FLORIDA

Fog Island
A Vancouver Island Circumnavigation Full of Surprises
Copyright ©2023 by Norm Colver

Published in the USA by:
Seaworthy Publications, Inc.
6300 N Wickham Rd.
#130-416
Melbourne, FL 32940
Phone 321-610-3634
email orders@seaworthy.com
www.seaworthy.com
Your Bahamas and Caribbean Cruising Advisory

Library of Congress Cataloging-in-Publication Data

Names: Culver, Norm, 1951- author.
Title: Fog island : a Vancouver Island circumnavigation full of surprises /
  Norm Culver.
Description: Melbourne, FL : Seaworthy Publications Inc., [2022] | Summary:
  "Vancouver Island stretches from Washington State almost halfway to
  Alaska and its west coast is exposed to the stormy and unpredictable
  North Pacific Ocean. This coast, known as the graveyard of the Pacific
  because of the great number of ships that have foundered here, is lined
  with rocks and often covered with fog. On this circumnavigation of the
  island nearly 50 years ago, there were few navigational instruments, so
  Norm and his crew had to grope through thick fog trying to find safe
  places to anchor. Sometimes they didn't see another boat or person for
  days and they ate what we could catch from the sea and find on the
  shores. It was a one-and-one-half month voyage in a small,
  trouble-ridden sailboat. Norm had no experience with this and had to
  learn things the hard way. However, they came across hidden totem poles,
  longhouses, and moss-covered skulls propped on rotting dugouts. They
  found a forty-foot beached whale still wiggling, heard wolves howling
  throughout the night, soaked bare in a spring that was so hot they could
  hardly crawl back out and they anchored alone in quiet bays with nothing
  but the ducks for company"-- Provided by publisher.
Identifiers: LCCN 2022039983 (print) | LCCN 2022039984 (ebook) | ISBN
  9781948494656 (paperback) | ISBN 9781948494663 (epub)
Subjects: LCSH: Culver, Norm, 1951---Travel--British Columbia--Vancouver
  Island. | Sailing--North Pacific Ocean. | Sailing--Georgia, Strait of
  (B.C. and Wash.) | Vancouver Island (B.C.)--Travel and description.
Classification: LCC F1089.V3 C85 2022 (print) | LCC F1089.V3 (ebook) |
  DDC 917.11/204--dc23/eng/20220929
LC record available at https://lccn.loc.gov/2022039983
LC ebook record available at https://lccn.loc.gov/2022039984

Once when I was young I spotted some wild ducks across the bay. I pushed off in a small rowboat and went after them. I followed them around a rocky point and into a narrow channel. Where the channel opened into several wooded islands and small inlets, I lost them. I searched and searched—and I've been looking for them ever since.

Table of Contents

PROLOGUE

The fog was thick. How thick? That's usually measured by the number of boat-lengths of visibility. But how do you do that in the middle of a black night when you can hardly see the water ahead? Worse yet, we were in a Pacific storm, waves crashing over the bow, and whipping the boat violently in every direction.

Clutching the rail with one hand and the tiller with the other, I squinted ahead for the sight of anything—another boat, land, rocks, whatever. Occasionally I honked the handheld horn, hoping any nearby boat would hear it, so that they wouldn't hit us. Those were the days before chart plotters and GPS. We navigated by what was called dead reckoning. That's where you try to keep track of your position by the compass and boat speed. But how do you do that with the compass whipping back and forth about 120 degrees with each wave? And how do you determine boat speed with the boat going about zero up the waves and about five knots down the waves? So how would we ever know when to turn into our destination of Barkley Sound?

The three of us were taking turns steering until the one at the tiller became too seasick to continue. When I turned the tiller over to Phil, I told him to steer about 300 degrees and I went below and crashed in a bunk. Those 300 degrees were intended to keep us away from the rocky shoreline on this treacherous West Coast of Vancouver Island. Instead, assuming I was being overcautious, Phil turned farther inland. Too far inland.

What happened next was the nearest I've ever come to a tragic death.

Without knowing it, we passed through a maze of rocks which is actually a part of Cape Beale. I awoke because it was suddenly calm. That's because we were just as suddenly off the rough ocean and inside the calm of Barkley Sound. I asked Phil what happened. He said he got too far in, and in the thick fog, big rocks suddenly appeared all around us. He said it was too late to turn back, so he steered as best he could, between the rocks.

In checking the chart of this, I'm sure anyone would agree that this was nothing short of a miracle.

This miraculous escape happened the year before my first circumnavigation of Vancouver Island. It proved to be a blessing in disguise. It taught me to not only take greater precautions, but to be prepared for unforeseen dangers we might not be able to avoid.

PREFACE

There's an underlying reason a person buys a boat, especially if he's a sailor. It's not just a boat that he's buying. It's a self-contained capsule, and in it he can find what he seeks, which is adventure. And with more knowledge and experience, he seeks a greater adventure, a bigger goal. A goal for which he can prepare meticulously. But he never eliminates the risk. Some of the risk is what makes for the adventure. It takes two things to fully live, nature and fear. Nature for renewal and fear for zest. And a voyage like this provides both. There's nothing like the fear of being lost in fog that brings out the zest for finding protection, and there's nothing like the raw nature of finding a quiet bay that brings out renewal.

So, I guess I'm a voyager. Through one of those many boating cuts, some saltwater must have leaked into my bloodstream. And it keeps circulating through me. And it must have come from the waters off Vancouver Island. And still at the age of 83, it keeps pulling me back, for voyage after voyage.

There's a vast coastline off Vancouver Island. It's a coastline that puts a voyager on his own. A distant speck may grow into what becomes a passing boat, and after it passes, his own capsule seems to shrink back into another speck.

In gales here a voyager must surf through waves so big he hates to look back at them, and in fog, he has to grope for a safe place to anchor.

There are gray whales here that blow, killer whales that roll, and tens of thousands of murres, auklets, and puffins that scurry away from the bow as it plunges through the seas. There are beaches where bears grind mussels for hours and hillsides where wolves howl throughout the night.

There's a bluff where over 200 years ago, Chief Maquinna watched Captain Cook make white man's first landing on this coast, where dozens of longhouses stood, and where some of the chief's descendants are still living.

There are ancient ruins surrounded by middens, where for ages natives ate clams beside their fires. And hidden in the brush behind one of these ruins are the remains of a longhouse with two totems poking out of the brush, one leaning and one face down. There's a small island with an Indian chief's burial ground and resting there on a rotting dugout, are three skulls—their sockets staring at you.

There's another island with a niche just big enough for a boat to anchor, and ashore there is a trail so overgrown with salal that a person must almost crawl to ingress. Beyond that there's an ocean beach that's jammed with a thousand drift logs and where a broad rocky point is covered with tide pools, all teaming with life, and where sea lions roar and eagles perch in storm-torn shreds of trees.

A bizarre boardwalk leads to a hot spring that flows right into the ocean and where a fatigued seafarer can soak bare while watching the troughs suck holes out of the rocky shore and the combers plunge them full.

There's a bay where loons yodel, kingfishers chatter, and thrushes flute their spiraling songs back and forth across the water. And where the sun, setting round and red, turns the trees on the opposite shore into a tall picket fence. And where lacy clouds go gray, then ink, and the dark blue sky goes yellow, then rose and the sunset becomes a deep orange. And then an immense twilight rises through the trees and turns the land to an eerie night-snow-gray.

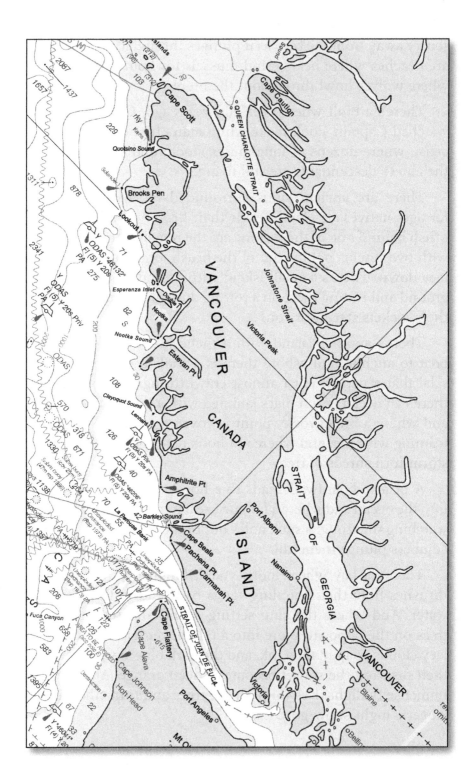

CHAPTER ONE
WE'RE OFF

A crackling voice on the VHF radio predicted the weather, "June 13th, Juan de Fuca Strait, winds east to southeasterly five to fifteen knots, increasing to twenty to thirty knots."

I'd heard those stronger wind forecasts before, but their maximums never seemed to materialize, especially in the summer. Assuming say fifteen or twenty knots, we figured that would make for a great sail across the strait—exactly what the boat was designed for.

I wanted to make the crossing to Victoria today even though it would mean arriving after dark. The general plan for our Vancouver Island circumnavigation was to make time going up the inside of the island in order to allow more time for the less accessible and more intriguing outside coast.

Juan de Fuca Strait, larger than Long Island Sound, funnels water like the neck of an hourglass between the Pacific Ocean and two inland seas—Puget Sound to the south and Georgia Strait to the north. Enough water flows through the strait for its tidal height to cover a house. In some of the narrow passes in the Georgia Strait area this flow of water actually cascades downhill causing rapids, and as stated in the British Columbia Coast Sailing Directions: *Dangerous overfalls, eddies, extremely violent whirlpools, and upwellings.* Such whirlpools can whip a boat twice our size end-for-end, throwing its crewmen to the deck. And the upwellings here can burst up with six-foot vertical walls of water. In Seymour Narrows for instance, water sometimes funnels through at over fifteen knots and that rush can create whirlpools powerful enough to suck large logs underwater and then erupt them from the upwellings. In order to avoid all this, we had to watch the current tables very carefully, because in a few days we would be traversing some of these places.

It was time to get underway. Because the wind and the waves were up more than we'd expected; Dale and I had to hang on for support when moving about and Mary Ann went below.

Dale and I put on our foul weather gear. We estimated the wind at over twenty-five knots, so we decided to set minimal sail. Dale headed the boat into the wind and cut the speed. I crept forward like a cat, and with an arm wrapped around the forward stay, attached the small jib. From the cockpit, Dale hoisted it, pulling and winching its halyard down tightly. Then he hoisted the mainsail, but only to a lower height. From the cabin top I tied down the reefing lines, fixing the sail at that level, and while Dale winched and cleated it there, I scooted back to the cockpit.

Dale reached into a compartment and pulled the bag of emergency supplies to the top where, if needed, we could more quickly get to it. The bag containing a radio beacon instrument, flares, and other rescue items, would go with us in the dinghy if we ever had to abandon ship.

Once the sails were set, we turned back on course with the direction of the wind. The sails blasted full, the aft rigging snapped taut, and the boat burst ahead. We attached our harness lines to solid parts of the boat. Without exchanging a word, we both knew from previous overboard practice, that if while unharnessed, either of us fell overboard, we wouldn't likely be rescued. I hoped Mary Ann would stay below. She couldn't swim well.

Out in the open water, the wind grew stronger. We didn't know its actual velocity because we didn't have a wind gauge, but there was a low howling. We felt the waves growing too, especially as we drew closer to Point Wilson. We couldn't see the size of the waves because it was getting dark and there was no moon. Occasionally, we saw barely illuminated by the bow lights, the shimmering crests on the waves. Sometimes we ducked spumes of water. The boat began twisting and jerking so that steering became more difficult.

We knew we had waited too long to leave Port Townsend. We were caught in the breaking waves of a chop. The knot meter, measuring our speed through the water, read about seven knots. But trying to judge our speed over the ground was more difficult. Instead, we watched to see how fast the streetlights of Port Townsend were moving backward, but because of the boat's pitching, that was hard to judge.

We needed to know what course to take once beyond Point Wilson, so gripping the chart under the hatch cover where it wouldn't blow away, and with the flashlight held in my teeth, I laid a straightened finger against the chart to guesstimate a course. About 310 degrees. I turned to the compass. It was spinning. I estimated about 300 degrees between its oscillations. Close enough.

By now I was holding the tiller with both hands, sometimes almost leaning on it. I remembered accounts of rudders breaking from such heavy stress. I couldn't help but wonder what if our rudder were to break. I figured we'd have to rig something like a board in order to steer the boat. But how would we do that in these conditions?

Then my bad thoughts strayed to a deadhead we'd passed earlier in the day. Deadheads are heavy logs that lie vertically, nearly sunken except for one end barely showing. If the boat ever came down on one, it could be like hitting a rock. I had to tell myself how extremely unlikely that was and that we were probably safer than riding in a car. I remembered that fact from a Power Squadron class where it was said that statistically, the most dangerous part of a boating weekend was driving to and from the boat. That thought helped.

As I turned the boat to port, some of the waves lurched her too far that way and I jerked the tiller back to avoid an accidental jibe, where the wind gets behind the mainsail and thrashes it to the other side of the boat. Even though we'd tied down the boom to prevent this from happening, I couldn't help some more *stinkin' thinkin'* about what would happen if this preventer line didn't hold and the boat broached, throwing it onto its side. I didn't know what it would take to broach a boat like this, but I had broached sailing dinghies, and when that happened, the wind flipped the dinghy so quickly all I remembered was ducking from the swinging boom and then being in the water, struggling to get back into the boat.

"Dale, look at Point Wilson. Does it seem like we're not gaining on it anymore?"

"Yeah. And with all this boat speed? What's going on here?"

"I don't know. The tables listed less than three knots of current here and that isn't even for a few hours. Anyway, I'm tired of this. Let's turn back."

Dale turned the boat back and onto a tack; and for the first time we were now headed into the wind and waves.

I grabbed a flashlight and shined it below. Mary Ann was holding onto a post with a blank stare. "We just turned back," I said. "And it's going to be rough for a while, but it will soon be over, and we'll be back to Port Townsend." Her eyes brightened some.

I knew that we had to be making progress now that we were going with the current, but I couldn't tell yet.

Our speed through the water meant nothing. We couldn't have been making much headway against the waves. I didn't even look at the knot meter to find out. Instead, I was looking back at the Point Wilson light. It was now moving rapidly away from us. We were making it.

While Dale took us back to Port Townsend, I went below and hugged Mary Ann.

"I didn't expect it to be so rough," she said.

"I didn't either," I answered. "But it's over, and from now on it shouldn't be this rough."

"Okay, I trust that you guys know what you're doing."

However, I wasn't so sure.

≈≈≈≈≈≈≈

We had departed Shilshole Bay earlier that day in our 29-foot sailboat, *Fog Island*, to begin a counterclockwise circumnavigation of Vancouver Island. After all the years of planning and preparation, we untied the boat, eased away from the dock and cheered, "We're off!"

This would be a one-and-a-half-month voyage, sailing several times the distance I'd ever sailed before and rounding that distant prize.

I had taken many local boating trips to the San Juan Islands, the Gulf Islands, and short distances beyond that. Then I began studying charts of more distant possibilities. The inland passage to Alaska intrigued me, but there was something that intrigued me even more. Extending halfway from Washington State to Alaska was this one huge island.

Islands are intriguing. They're set aside and isolated from the ordinary. In fact, the word, "isolate" is derived from French, Italian, and Latin, meaning "island." I look at an island like a climber looks at a mountain. But instead of just conquering it, I want to absorb it completely, seeing its entire shoreline, from start to finish, to be sure I haven't missed anything.

The more remote the island, the more complicated its circumnavigation, the more intrigued I am. This huge Canadian island I contemplated rounding had an ocean coastline that was not only remote but extensive. There are so many inlets, bays, and surrounding islands, it would be hard to count them all, let alone explore them. In fact, to closely follow this shoreline would require traveling about 25 times farther than a simple circumnavigation—and that's about twice the distance across all of Canada.

Vancouver Island is the largest Pacific Island in North America—285 miles long and 62 miles wide, with an area of 12,408 square miles. That's nearly half the size of Canada's New Brunswick province and almost twice the land area of all the Hawaiian Islands. It is half again larger than either of the states of New Jersey or Massachusetts and a third again larger than Vermont or New Hampshire. The islands length is approximately the distance from New York City to Buffalo or Toronto to Montreal and half the distance from Chicago to Atlanta.

With its irregular, lumpy borders, Vancouver Island is shaped like a long potato, extending half the length of the Canadian west coast. The island is mashed against the mainland, almost connected to it by a thick umbilical composed of a maze of small islands and a spiderweb of narrow channels. The water south of the umbilical is the Strait of Georgia, and Queen Charlotte Strait is north of it.

Despite its proximity to the mainland, the island is not easy to circumnavigate. Only a tiny percent of the local boaters have done it. An immense and effective barrier—the stormy and unpredictable North Pacific Ocean—surrounds most of the island. The coastline is rocky, often covered with fog, and because of the great number of ships that have wrecked and sunk here over the last 200 years, it is called the *Graveyard of the Pacific*.

Most of the island's interior is heavily forested, much of it is raw wilderness. Almost all the islands roughly three-quarter-million inhabitants reside along its coastline. In fact, about 95 percent of that population is clustered along only one-fourth of the coast between Sooke and Campbell River on the island's more protected southeastern portion. Victoria alone, on the tip of the island and the capital of British Columbia, contains about half of the island's population.

The remaining Vancouver Island inhabitants reside in isolated settlements along the rest of the coast and in the inlets. These settlements are up to dozens of miles apart and many have no roads connecting them. Traveling by water and measured in nautical miles, which are about 20 percent longer than land miles, it is 53 miles from Bull Harbor, the northernmost anchorage on the east coast, around the island's northwest end, to Winter Harbor on the west coast. Between these two harbors there are not only no inhabitants, but only one other harbor and that one is unsafe to enter in bad weather. Yet it is along this expanse that a boat must pass two of Vancouver Island's greatest obstacles: Nahwitti Bar, with sometimes steep breaking waves, and Cape Scott, the exposed north end of the island.

Continuing south from Winter Harbor, many of the settlements have neither boat repair nor medical facilities. Some have neither fuel nor supplies and from year-to-year, all these things can change.

≈ ≈ ≈ ≈ ≈ ≈ ≈

While Dale steered, I went below and rifled through some of the shelves and compartments to be doubly sure that we were self-contained enough for anything we'd likely encounter on the voyage.

When the wind increased enough to sail, I insisted on removing the mainsail cover myself. Smiling, I folded it into a neat bundle and stowed it in the least accessible compartment on the boat, where it would remain, leaving that sail always ready to use, for several times longer than ever before.

We raised both the mainsail and the jib, killed the noisy motor, and as the sails filled with wind, I felt the same thrill as when I raised my first canvas on a rowboat as a boy.

What a contrast the two of them were, sitting there in the cockpit. Dale, an experienced sailor, stood tall and husky with black hair covering most of his head and face and showing above his open shirt, resembling a contented bear. And Mary Ann, with no sailing experience, her delicate face barely exposed through the opening of her parka and wisps of her fine blonde hair blowing around, looked like a misplaced southern belle, which she now actually was. With long dark hair blowing in the wind, I stood there steering the boat—with a smile.

I looked over some details on the chart. It was the first of thirty-eight charts, stacked neatly in the order we'd be using them. Nothing more than heavy sheets of paper colored with yellow, blue, and white details, these charts would be our primary navigational guides throughout the voyage. I'd been studying them for months, sometimes even falling asleep gazing at one and dreaming of exploring its bays and channels, and then awakening the next morning to peer at it again.

Our speed was five knots. With my hand stretched against the chart, calculating a distance of five nautical miles between the ends of my thumb and middle finger, I measured off those distances from our present position to Port Townsend. With steady wind, each hand's distance would be one hour's sailing time. In three hours we would arrive at Port Townsend, our first planned stop. Our first navigation was accomplished, and our capsule was functioning well with nothing but wind for power.

Then I looked back toward Seattle—and my face went blank. I was leaving home for a trip that I didn't have to take. I needed to support my family, yet I wouldn't be working for a month and a half. How much would this absence affect my dental practice and how busy would it be when I returned?

But I needed an escape from the practice. Smiling, I'd put a sign on the door, "Office closed until August 1st." I disliked my own profession. The stress of it had overpowered the rewards. I felt burned out and wanted to quit but couldn't afford to.

For years I had enjoyed dental practice, but it had become more like work and production. What little fun remaining was overpowered by business turmoil. I thought however, how I had always enjoyed handcrafts. Why couldn't I approach dentistry the same way? The way a woodcraftsman enjoys his creative works. I decided to think more about that along the way and to write down my thoughts.

Next I thought of my three children's forced smiles and their quiet goodbyes as they left town with their mother before my trip. Over the last several years the fights with my wife had become so serious that I couldn't take it any longer. But my son was only two years old then and I just couldn't leave my "little man." So, I waited, and when he was five and things were no better, my wife and I separated, and I moved to live on the boat.

I was sick for myself too. I knew I wouldn't be living with my kids anymore and I didn't even know when I'd see them next. I worried also that I might never find another woman to be happy with.

Then I looked at Mary Ann. She was sitting there smiling at me. And my bad thoughts disappeared. We had met some years before in a Georgia park where I took daily walks during a vacation trip. I remembered the quiet way she looked at me when we said goodbye. After that I phoned her periodically when my marital problems became worse. Our talks helped. I decided to ask her to go on part of the boat trip. She admitted she had no sailing experience, but said she'd inquire about getting time off from the restaurant-club that she managed and

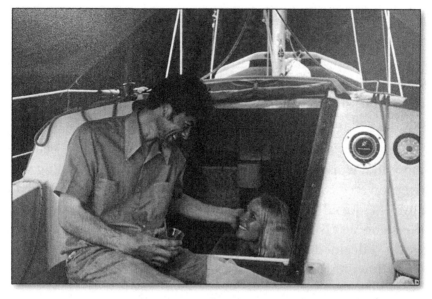

Norm and Mary Ann

about leaving her children with her sister. It worked. She could go.

After the sails were set and it was starting to warm up, I got three beers from the cooler and sat down beside Mary Ann.

"Hey, Norm..." Dale said. "Don't I get that other beer?"

"Oh God Dale. How could I forget my partner?"

Soon after purchasing the boat, I had remorse over its expense, and in order to share that expense, I decided to try to get a partner for it. The cost of the boat was $20,250, which in the 1970s was a heavy expense for me. Dale answered an ad I placed in the newspaper, and we agreed on a partnership. On this particular trip however, even though he was half owner, he was aboard as my crew. An aerospace engineer, Dale had a high-end job designing rocket engines. Yet he was unassuming, soft-spoken and genuine. Our partnership was working well, and we were becoming good friends.

As she sipped her beer, Mary Ann began to shiver. This was her first trip to the Northwest and because I had told her that her portion of the voyage would be in what we call the "banana belt," she'd brought only light clothing. To a northwesterner, this area in the lee of the Olympic and Vancouver Island Mountains is relatively warm, but she pointed to the surrounding snowy mountains and said, "Warm? That's a joke."

In the increasing wind the boat started rushing and sliding gracefully through the waves. Her tall mast, flat bottom and heavy keel made her sail fast and upright. And steering to dodge the occasional logs, she responded quickly.

Alone a shoreline, nearly barren from a million years of facing Juan de Fuca Strait, the wind was forcing quick patterns in the scrubby shore grass and storm-tossed logs, jumbled like sticks, cluttered the high-tide line.

After docking in Port Townsend, we roamed the streets and gawked at the ornate historic buildings. It felt like something out of Shakespeare. This was once the major lumbering hub of the Pacific Northwest, and two generations before, square-rigged sailing vessels lay at anchor here, crowding the harbor. We found a restaurant, ordered, and talked of our pleasant day and of the adventures ahead. We relaxed with coffee after dinner but watched how the wind was bending the trees more against the darkening sky.

Little did we know what the rest of the voyage held for us.

CHAPTER TWO

THE DREAM

As I contemplated a Vancouver Island circumnavigation, I first wondered if I was capable of doing it. My background seemed suited. As a high school teacher as well as a naturalist, my father was instrumental in starting high school conservation classes in Washington State; so, as a boy, I grew up at home in the outdoors. And as an older brother I learned to do things alone, so I didn't mind the idea of being alone on part of the Vancouver Island trip.

I also grew up with boats. Our family spent our summers at a small lake where my parents had purchased property when I was three years old. Then I was learning to row in a leaky, wood-planked boat tethered with a fifty-foot rope. At the age of twelve, after reading in a dusty old book about sailboats with old-fashioned, gaff-rigged sails, my dad let me rig our rowboat with that kind of a sail. I attached a piece of canvas to fir poles I'd cut and peeled myself and whenever the wind blew hard enough, I hoisted the apparatus, sailed across the lake, jerked the sail down just before hitting the fallen snags along the far shore and rowed back and did it again.

However, even after 40 more years of boating, I knew that a circumnavigation of Vancouver Island was a very different story. There would be plenty of unknowns and dangers. Half the trip would be on the open ocean which I'd hardly sailed at all before. I knew that I was inexperienced for this kind of a voyage. How would I prepare? I learned that one of the leaders of the local Power Squadron knew as much about this as anybody.

So, I phoned him and asked how big a boat he thought I ought to have for the trip.

In a gruff monotone, Mr. Gardner answered. "It's not the size of the boat but the design that counts."

"Okay, what features should I look for?" I asked.

"Well…" he chuckled. "Lots of things. For instance, a sailboat should have a good bridge deck. That's the raised portion between the cockpit and the cabin. That's so that if a wave breaks over the transom, it won't fill the cabin with water and sink the boat."

"Oh. I'll have to do some investigating. What am I likely to have problems with going around Vancouver Island?"

"Rocks, mainly."

"Can't you use the charts and look out for them?"

"That's fine inland, but what happens on the ocean when you're in fog and you hit one at the bottom of a big wave?"

"Well, how do you suggest I prepare for it."

"Take A.P."

"What's that?"

"The Power Squadron's Advanced Piloting class. It will give you all you need to get around the island and more."

Before taking the A.P. class, I took a prerequisite Advanced Piloting class which covered propulsion systems, hull design and construction, stability and trim, boat handling, docking, piloting, locking, trailering, anchoring, marlinspike seamanship, adverse conditions, stranding, towing, damage control, rescue, fire prevention and control, lay-up, fitting out, repairs, flag etiquette, and Customs rules.

After this prerequisite, I signed up for the Advanced Piloting class. It was an eight-month class and it turned out to be about as difficult as any college classes I'd ever taken, but it did build my confidence in boating. Following the A.P. class, I took two additional classes, "Weather for the Mariner" and "Celestial Navigation"—all to further prepare for the planned Vancouver Island trip.

My crew members for the trip, besides Mary Ann, would be six sailing friends who would exchange places, one or two at a time, at planned points along the route. There would be four such legs to the trip and two periods where I'd be alone. With some reluctance, I sent each of these upcoming crewmen the following letter.

Vancouver Island crew:

Things look great for the trip, but mainly for safety I want to set up some rules.

1. Know how to read charts and don't get anywhere near rocks, especially when it's rough. Know how to take compass bearings and keep track of our position because when you're at the helm, you're responsible.

2. When steering, watch for logs and especially deadheads. Hitting a deadhead in rough water could be "all she wrote."

3. Before getting into fog or any potential danger, let me know even if I'm below. Before entering fog, we'll take a fix of our position, run by dead reckoning (keeping track of speed, compass course, and time), reduce speed, use lights, maybe have a bow watch and sound the horn every minute or two. The accuracy of our steering and dead reckoning may be what keeps us off the rocks. Unless we're certain of our position, we'll probably wait out heavy fog at sea rather than risk approaching land.

4. To prevent falling overboard at night or in bad weather, harness yourself to the boat. Take all precautions not to fall overboard. If you do, consider it your own fault,

and even though we'll have practiced man-overboard routines, under rough conditions recovery is not always possible.

5. Know how to use the VHF radio, which is the main safety item aboard.

6. Know how to use the two burner alcohol stove, which can be a serious hazard.

7. Our fuel tank only holds fifteen gallons so we'll run at about half throttle, which is about all the power needed to make the boat's hull speed, and that amount of fuel will then take us about one hundred miles—when there isn't enough wind to sail. The motor is an atomic four (commonly called an atomic bomb, because of its problems). It's a four-cylinder 30 horsepower gasoline engine.

8. Food will be simple. If you don't like something, instead of complaining, fix your own. Give me your preferences of food and alcohol beforehand. We'll get most food before leaving, and because of Customs limits for alcohol, most of that will be gotten in Canada.

9. We won't have regular steering watches because there shouldn't be many long, nonstop stretches. Instead, share watches voluntarily and when you're tired of steering just ask someone else to take over. We'll also share cooking, washing dishes, cleaning, and other chores informally.

10. Because of our twenty-one-gallon water capacity, use fresh water only for cooking and drinking and saltwater for everything else including bathing and washing dishes.

11. Keep your personal gear to a minimum.

12. Even though you may think I'm a son-of-a-bitch, I'll make some of the final decisions.

Meeting and overboard drill next Saturday, 4:00 p.m. at the dock.

Captain Bligh

Despite the blunt letter, everyone showed up for the meeting and the overboard drill. Each of us practiced using the radio for mayday emergencies and we even tried a collision mat that I'd read about, and which Captain Cook used to save his ship when it struck the Great Barrier Reef off Australia. To do this we lowered a weighted canvas mat, and with attached lines, pulled it under the bow as we would have to do in order to cover a hole in the hull.

Most of our time, however, was spent with the overboard drills. Single-handedly, each of us took turns recovering a cushion dummy thrown into the water. Steering when he could, the one practicing had to throw the life ring and overboard pole toward the dummy, then start the motor and either lower or slacken the sails and return to the dummy as quickly as possible. Then, passing closely by the dummy, the person practicing had to fish it out of the water with a boat hook as he would try to do if it were an actual person overboard.

These drills did not turn out to be as easy as we'd thought. Twice the life ring jammed such that it couldn't be thrown into the water and the same thing happened once with the overboard pole. Another time the life ring was mistakenly thrown into the towed dinghy. Another time the motor didn't start and yet another time it died during a recovery. Almost every time, the sails thrashed and the lines tangled, so that it was difficult to steer. We did, however, have some fun. While each of the guys toiled at his turn, the rest of us cheered and booed his performance.

During the drills, one bad accident happened. In fact, it was one of the worst things that can happen when sailing. In an accidental jibe, in which the mainsail thrashed uncontrollably across the cockpit, the metal boom smashed into Phil's head with a loud bang and tore his scalp open. But even with blood gushing from his scalp, he was so intent on completing his drill, we couldn't get him to stop until he looked down and saw that the white boat was turning red. So, we sat him down, taped the wound closed and continued the drills.

Some of the recoveries of the dummy took several passes and up to twenty minutes to complete. In that time a person in the cold Northwest water would have become hypothermic. And rather than the light wind and low waves in which we were practicing, the conditions under which a person would have most likely actually fallen overboard, would have been rough. Furthermore, we had no deadweight that could be used to resemble a possibly unconscious person we needed to haul from the water.

Because of such risks, my excitement about the adventure was clouded with some worry. In fact, the day before leaving, I was depressed, and secretly even contemplated changing my mind about the whole trip.

My stepfather had warned me about the dangers of the waters off Vancouver Island. As a young man he fished commercially on his forty-three-foot boat in Alaska and Washington and traveled around Vancouver Island. That was back in the thirties before the days of any electronic equipment, when water depth was measured like Mark Twain did, with a hand thrown, weighted line.

Once while he was in the vicinity, a U.S. Navy warship sustained extensive damage hitting a rock while passing through Seymour Narrows in an adverse current. Yet our small plastic boat might soon be passing through the same narrows.

Another time, while fishing off the coast of Vancouver Island with his brother, they watched, horrified, as one huge crested rogue wave came at them. There was no way to escape it. They slowed the boat, headed toward the wave, and hoped. The wave tore over the whole boat, but luckily the cabin was still intact, and the boat was still floating. His brother never went fishing again.

The boat I purchased for the circumnavigation was a 29-foot Ranger sailboat. She was designed for both racing and cruising, however because my main focus was on the voyage, I never seriously raced her. Even so, I wanted a faster, more responsive boat. I'd sailed some slow dogs before and found them to be not much fun. Unfortunately, however, the lighter boat would turn out to be bouncier and not even as seaworthy in the heavier sea conditions we would encounter on the trip.

After two years of sailing and preparing her, I had checked, adjusted or improved everything from the masthead fittings to the keel bottom. I had literally checked every nut, bolt, and screw I could find.

I provisioned the boat for any likely occurrence I knew of. Each item on my seven-page checklist was checked off. For instance, the boat carried a medical kit with adrenaline, penicillin, Demerol, syringes and a tourniquet, surgical knife, resusitube, and even a tracheotomy kit. As a dentist, I knew of these medical items, and being detail oriented I learned about the other items. In fact, both dentists and sailors tend to be perfectionistic little bastards, so, I was the worst combination.

My plan was to circumnavigate the island counterclockwise. I'd heard and read that that was the preferred route because most of the repair facilities are on the inside of the island where they're more likely to be needed during the early, shakedown period. The route was also said to be preferred because of the typical winds. The inside of the island is protected from strong ocean winds and while traveling south down the outside, the open ocean is supposed to offer good sailing with the prevailing summer north-westerlies.

On our voyage, none of this was to work out. Instead of sailing up the inside in protection, that's where we were to encounter our strongest northwesterlies funneling even stronger down

Fog Island

some of the long passages. And instead of running down the outside with the predicted ocean northwesterlies, that's where we were to fight our worst southerlies.

Getting most repairs done on the inside of the island wasn't to work out either. Most of our breakdowns were to occur on the outside, when the ocean got rough and where there were the fewest people and fewer yet repair facilities.

I planned on leaving early in the summer to avoid most of the fog. Fog is supposed to increase dramatically as the summer progresses. Statistics for the West Coast of Vancouver Island show that July has about twice as many foggy days as June, and August has about twice again as many as July. (That's why August is often called "Fogust.") Even though the usual weather is stormier earlier in the summer, I chanced for that rather than more fog.

None of this was to work out either. Instead, we were to get not only lots of stormy weather, but lots of fog as well. In fact, my naming the boat Fog Island turned out to be just right.

CHAPTER THREE

RIPTIDE

*A*fter the first night's roughness, we asked ourselves in the morning, "Where did we go wrong?"

We checked the chart and current tables again and found something we hadn't noticed before. In the current tables there was a detailed portion called Current Differences, which showed that the current at Point Wilson was two times the 2.7 knots listed for the rest of Admiralty Inlet. Even that however, didn't explain the greater strength of the current we seem to have encountered.

We talked with the dock attendant. He said he'd seen us leave the night before and wondered if we'd make it around the point. He told us that the current there sometimes runs at twelve knots. I said the tables only listed about five and he answered, "I know. That's wrong."

He also told us that the night's wind had reached thirty-nine knots. That didn't surprise us. We were in it.

By coincidence, we had encountered the combination of an abnormally strong summer storm which was against an abnormally strong current—a sailor's nightmare. We talked it over. Nothing like that should happen again, right? Today we would try again to do what we'd failed to do the night before: cross twenty-five-mile-wide Juan de Fuca Strait.

In these early summer periods when the moon is high in the Pacific Northwest, it exerts a strong gravitational pull on the water and that creates big differences between high and low tides, along with strong currents. On the opposite side of the globe, there's a reciprocal bulge of water with equally big tides and strong currents. When the earth revolves halfway between however, the Northwest is then positioned north of that bulge and its tidal differences are decreased, and its currents weaken. The result, known as mixed tide, is an alternating strong ebb and flood current followed by a weak ebb and flood. The strong current we had encountered the night before would therefore be followed by a weak one this morning.

Before leaving we wanted to know what the current would be doing once we reached the other side of the strait. The current tables for Race Rocks, not far from Victoria, showed that by the time we'd be there it would be ebbing at about three knots. That wouldn't affect us much because it would be running more or less sideways to our course.

The wind forecast was downgraded, and the treetops were barely swaying. The storm seemed to be over.

Though we agreed conditions were much more favorable, we delayed breakfast over more coffee. We just didn't feel like venturing out yet. Finally, after cleaning up the mess from where things were tossed the night before, Dale and I hauled the dinghy onto the dock and dumped out the water left in it. Before putting it back in the water, we decided to pull its drain plug. Though this would let some water in, we figured it would allow the water to drain out when it was being towed, which would prevent it from filling in bad weather as had happened the day before.

Over another cup of coffee, I studied the chart of the strait once more, examining every detail within a wide zone of our planned route. There were no other warnings, so we stowed things for the crossing—but before departing, I cautiously asked, "Well, are the two of you ready to go?"

"Sure," Dale answered.

"Yes!" Mary Ann answered. "But only if we can turn back if it gets rough."

"I couldn't agree more," I stressed.

And we departed.

We could hardly believe the contrast from the night before. The current at Point Wilson was barely noticeable and the water nearly flat. By late morning enough wind came up to sail, so we set full sail and steered for Victoria. But instead of seeing Vancouver Island ahead, we only saw low clouds. Or perhaps it was fog.

In case of fog, we would try to determine our position by dead reckoning—where you keep track of time, speed, and heading—though I'd had little experience actually doing it. Also, we would use the radio direction finder (RDF) to help navigate across the strait—and then try to enter Victoria's Oak Bay by listening to the foghorns and matching our depth soundings with the depths marked on the chart.

"Let's try the RDF," I suggested. "We might need it. We're in open water now and there are several beacons around here."

I went below where we had the RDF placed on the table and strapped to a bulkhead. From a sketch of radio beacons we had taped behind it, I found beacons at Point Wilson, Dungeness, Race Rocks, and Smith Island; they were all broadcast on the same frequency—314. I dialed the RDF to that frequency and tuned into the Morse code that was being broadcast there. After asking Dale to steer as straight as possible, I played with the RDF—for what would be its first acid test.

Sure enough, just as was listed for Point Wilson's beacon, dah-dah dit-dah was being broadcast repeatedly. Then it changed to dah-dah dit, Smith Island's beacon, and so on. With each signal, I spun the circular radio antenna to the direction of the weakest sound and wrote down those compass bearings. Then I compared those bearings with the known ones from the chart.

They matched! At least closely. In case of fog, this meant we'd be able to determine our approximate position. From below I asked Dale and Mary Ann if they could see either Dungeness or Smith Island. They couldn't. But on our new machine, I could.

Once in the open strait we ran downwind free and fast under full sail—faster down the backs of the bigger waves. We also began to feel the rise and fall of swells coming in from the ocean and rolling down the entire nearly one-hundred-mile length of Juan de Fuca Strait. The increasing waves and swells tried to roll and pitch *Fog Island,* but her flat bottom reacted to each lurch with a quick reassuring uprighting surge, kind of like a dune buggy on bumpy sand.

Smith Island emerged from the clouds to our starboard. Unlike other islands of the Pacific Northwest, Smith Island is more of a reef, like you'd expect to see in the Bahamas. At the extreme end of Juan de Fuca Strait, this barren island catches the full fury of every ocean storm that funnels down the strait. No wonder it's been so leveled.

To our port, we began to make out Dungeness Spit. A sand spit measuring only a few feet in elevation, this spit arches out and eastward a distance of four miles. The water inside the spit is so shallow that at low tide, a tall person can walk the approximate mile across its inner bay.

Midway across the strait, Lopez Island became visible. Lopez is the southern-most major island of the 174 San Juan Islands, where inside the protection of these popular islands, I had enjoyed many sunny trips learning to sail.

Ahead, the lower clouds grew darker and more distinct. We soon distinguished it as land. Yes there it was, the southeastern end of Vancouver Island. The end of the big island which, if things went as planned, I would be seeing again after the long circumnavigation.

The wind had increased to over 25 knots and was blowing steadily. We were flying fast enough through the water that we needed to reduce sails. Dale and I went into our routine. He turned the boat into the wind, and while harnessed in, I went to the bow, dragging along with me the bag containing the smaller jib sail. As I was tugging the bigger jib down and hooking the smaller one on, the bow rhythmically rose like an elevator and fell almost weightlessly. But just before plunging underwater at the bottom of each fall, the bow stopped, with the water sometimes only inches from my feet. Once I realized I wasn't going to be washed overboard, I started enjoying the ride.

We also reefed the mainsail to a reduced size and then turned back on course. Even with the smaller sails, *Fog Island* was rushing down the growing waves at six to seven knots and gaining an eagle's view on their crests.

Mary Ann looked behind us. "Look how big the waves are!" she exclaimed. "They look like they'll bury us."

I hadn't been looking back, so I did then, and it was just as we sank into a trough that was so deep I had to twist my head up to see the top of the next onrushing crest coming directly at us immediately behind the transom. I braced, clutched the boat and at the last instant the stern rose rapidly right up the face of the wave, and as though nothing had happened, it was gone.

"Damn, Mary Ann, you're right about those waves."

"Yeah, it's kind of scary," she said. "But it's kind of fun too, once you realize you're not going to get eaten by them."

Looking back again, I hollered, "Where's the radio antenna?"

Where we'd repaired it the day before with duct tape, a wave must have ripped it apart and it was dragging through the water by its cable. When the next wave floated it high enough, I fished it out of the water and tied it down on the deck. That meant however, that there would probably be no radio reception from now on.

Crouched and tense, Dale was steering like a race car driver steering through a pack of race cars. I offered to spell him and found that dodging the steepest waves was indeed a challenge.

Discovery Island lay dead ahead. The buildings of Victoria behind it were getting larger. And in front of Discovery Island the water began to look peculiar. It was white and seemed elevated. We couldn't steady the binoculars well enough to see what it was. We had to wait, watching and wondering. As we drew closer we saw what it was—a seething fury of steep breaking waves.

"What in the world. Ever seen anything like that Dale?"

Luckily, Mary Ann was below then and didn't see it. A strong current coming down Haro Strait from the north must have been obliquely meeting an equally strong current in Juan de Fuca Strait. And where they met, the water was literally exploding. A riptide—and one like I'd never seen before.

"God, how can we get out of this Dale? Let's forget Victoria. Let's just try to get around this thing."

"But how?" Dale answered.

We couldn't turn back. The current seemed to be sucking us toward the rip faster than we'd be able to make headway going against it. We couldn't turn right either. That was Haro Strait, and I knew how strong the current there could be. Once I'd tried to buck it and moved so slowly I counted the branches on one tree for half an hour. We couldn't turn left because the growing rip was about as bad in that direction.

We were trapped. We had no choice but to go through it. We had to plan quickly. Once in the riptide, I didn't know if we'd be able to control the boat, let alone navigate. I grabbed the chart and tried to read it through the spray. Plumper Passage looked like the safest route to Victoria, but it had submerged rocks on both sides of its entrance. There wasn't time now to determine just where those rocks were. When the time came I hoped we'd be able to see where they were from waves breaking over them. But would breaking waves show through this inferno?

We were speeding toward the rip. *Fog Island* was bursting and crashing through the waves. My grip on the tiller tightened, as much to keep my footing as to maintain some control of the boat.

"We've got to reduce sail even more. Right away, Dale!"

I hollered below to Mary Ann, "It's going to get rougher for a while. Hang on tight."

I checked my harness. Still tightly attached.

I pushed the tiller hard to port. The sails slapped deafeningly. Dale, harnessed to the mast, un-cleated the halyard and jerked down on the mainsail. It didn't give much. A wave threw the bow aside. Wind caught the sails and they banged taut. Again, I fought to get the bow upwind. Dale yanked harder on the mainsail. This time he got more of it down. We couldn't reef the sail down properly under these conditions so he strung part of the halyard around as much of it as he could and tied it there. Loose flaps of the sail thrashed but at least for now it stayed tied down, out of the wind.

The boom thrashed with the sail. I heard a snap. The block holding the boom to the boat had broken. I tried to tighten the sheet enough to stop the thrashing and hoped that that would prevent the block from breaking completely off. If it did, who knows what the free-flying boom would smash into.

While Dale was inching back to the cockpit, I had to let go of the tiller so that I could tie down the broken block. With the tiller unmanned, I jumped up, straddling the cockpit as far forward as my harness would pull, and threw another line around as much of the flapping sail as I could reach. While tightening the line with my hands and teeth, wind caught in the jib and threw the bow downwind again. With only the small jib and the loose peak of the main exposed, *Fog Island* sailed herself more or less downwind, but erratically.

We could do nothing more. We watched it coming. It didn't build gradually but jutted up vertically out of the sea like a wall. A wall of froth. Like a cauldron of white flames lashing at each other, without pattern. Silently, I asked for help.

We struck it like a collision. The bow shot up and went airborne. I fell backwards, partly hanging by my harness line. Dale hung on with both hands. The bow fell onto another wave with a crash. The boat jolted left, then right. The mast whipped.

We tried to steer, but it didn't seem to help. The tiller was just something to hang onto.

Torrents of water gushed over the deck. Even with the hatch closed, I wasn't sure how much water might have been getting into the cabin. In what seemed like forever, but was probably only a few minutes, the cauldron eased. I slithered back to the tiller and steered away from the waves ahead that were apparently breaking over the rocks off Discovery Island.

"Mary Ann, it's over," I hollered below. "Thank God it's over." She looked up from the floor and said nothing.

Just as suddenly, the sea flattened to mere three-foot waves.

While Dale steered, navigating us past the rocks, he hollered, "We made it! What a boat this is!"

I whispered, "Thank You."

I went below and helped Mary Ann to her feet and out into the cockpit.

She whispered something and stared ahead.

"How was it?" I asked her.

"Terrible. I just wanted it to be over and to get to land."

"I know."

"I was afraid the boat would tip over. The waves were so scary thru the windows. It looked like we were in a whirlpool."

"Yes, it was awful. Worst I've ever seen."

"Norm, what about the pilot?" Dale asked. "If that kind of a riptide isn't marked on the chart, is there anything written about it in the pilot?"

"I don't know. Before the trip, I read up on everything but just for the areas north of here—because I'd been here before and it was always easy."

I went below and read aloud from the pilot (British Columbia Sailing Directions): "In the vicinity of Discovery Island tidal streams attain a considerable rate, and cause heavy tide rips which, except in calm weather, are dangerous to small craft."

"Why the hell isn't this on the chart?" I shouted.

"Maybe it's on the newer ones." Dale suggested. "Or on the more detailed ones that we don't have."

After winding our way through the rocks and reef-surrounded entrance channel, there it was. What a blessed sight, after all we'd been through. Docks full of boats—Victoria's Oak Bay Marina.

An older, weathered attendant met us at the Customs, dock and with a grimace, asked, "How was it out there?"

I paused, pondering playing down the roughness to this tough old hand and Mary Ann blurted, "Terrible!"

"Musta been," he said. "Worst summer storm I've ever seen. A freak situation to have such a strong southeaster this time of year. When you see waves breaking over the point out there, you know it's rough."

The three of us flopped on the cockpit seats.

"It's over," Dale said.

"Thank God," Mary Ann answered.

"And it should be over for the rest of the trip," I added.

"I hope you're right," Mary Ann said.

"Sorry about this roughness, Mary Ann," I said. "I really had no idea it would be this bad, especially on your part of the trip."

I just sat there, wondering what she was thinking. Like questioning her decision of going on the boat trip, and maybe pondering jumping ship now. She was staring down with a blank face at an apple in her lap.

Then, after pausing, she took a bite of the apple, looked back at me and said between chomps, "Actually there were some good parts of the trip. Things like I never would have seen otherwise. And yes, from here on things look more peaceful. You promise that?"

I smirked and said, "Yes, I promise. Otherwise, the two of you can throw me overboard. Deal...?"

Clearing Canadian Customs went well—except for one thing. Apples aren't allowed to be taken into Canada. But the woman Customs officer, perhaps picking up on Mary Ann's look of disappointment, cut each of our remaining apples open, removed the cores and seeds and let us keep the rest.

Before clearing Customs however, I was concerned—because things had not always gone this well. Once one of my crewmen jumped off the boat the minute we arrived at the dock and headed off for a walk. Customs rules strictly prohibit this. No one is allowed to leave a boat until it has fully cleared Customs. When the Customs officer arrived at our boat, he told us about breaking the rules, and said he could have our boat confiscated. I gulped, apologized profusely and after a long, agonizing delay (and after my crewmen returned to the boat), the officer finally let us go.

Another time, one of my daughters was aboard when I was wondering about the possibility of her experimenting with drugs. When the Customs officer asked if we had anything aboard that wasn't allowed, I blundered and said that we had no drugs aboard. With that, two Customs people took about an hour searching every nook and cranny on the boat and spread out every speck of our belongings. Thankfully, no drugs were found. Though she got the message of how serious drugs can be, my daughter and I have laughed about that one ever since.

Customs supervisors have especially awesome power. Once, when I was dating a Canadian woman and we were driving back and forth across the border to see one another, I phoned a U.S. Customs supervisor about some complications she was having in all these border crossings. I happened to tell him about some problems that were developing in our relationship—and this is exactly what he said.

"Do you want us to keep her out of the country for you?"

Flabbergasted, and after a long pause, I said, "Thank you so much, sir, but things aren't that bad."

"Just let us know," he answered.

CHAPTER FOUR
THRILLING ROUTE NORTH

In the morning I awoke with a jolt. I saw yesterday's riptide. But I said nothing. In fact, none of us said much before breakfast.

I broke the ice. "I'm so sorry about these last two days. Everything went wrong. But now we're past all that. Really. It can't happen again—or at least for the rest of the time you two are aboard. In fact, it should be the opposite. Today we'll be in the Gulf Islands—and they're totally protected."

After a long pause, Dale guardedly agreed with me. Mary Ann put on a brave face and calmly said she had confidence we'd be okay from now on.

Before departing we needed to repair the radio antenna which had broken in the riptide. Using scrap pieces of metal for support and plenty of duct tape, we jury-rigged a repair and smirked at it.

Ahead looked like some fog. With land close to us now, I wanted to be sure the compass was accurate. So, we did what's called swinging the compass. That's where you check the compass heading against known headings, like between two points of land, in order to determine if there's any deviation of the compass caused by metal on the boat. So, with Mary Ann steering the boat between a few such points, I checked the compass and Dale wrote down those headings. Luckily, we found no deviation or at least nothing to worry about.

The formula for this is TVMDC, and there's a (not very nice) saying for remembering the formula: True Virgins Make Dull Company. The formula means that true north (T in the formula), plus or minus variation (V), which is caused by the earth's magnetism, equals magnetic north (M). And M, plus or minus deviation (D), from any magnetism on the boat, equals compass north (C), which is what's actually shown on the compass. So, for our location, 360 degrees (T), minus the 21 degrees of easterly variation (V), equals 339 degrees magnetic (M); and this 339 degrees, plus or minus deviation (D)—which in this case was zero, still equals 339 degrees compass north (C).

Interestingly, one part of this formula, variation (which by the way is now usually called declination) changes over time. That's because the earth's magnetism changes over time. Now, instead of 21 degrees for our location, as it was when we took this trip, it is 18 degrees.

Once this drill was completed and we knew that the compass was accurate, we relaxed, feeling more confident in case of fog. More than that, we were especially relaxed because we were now sailing along in the glory of these protected waters. In fact, the trauma of the last two days was fading away.

After hours of steering, we improvised a "self-steering" system. We looped a rope loosely around the tiller with its ends tied to cleats on both side of the boat. This way we could snug the loop tight around the tiller by pulling it aft, and this held the boat on that course, at least for a while. This gave us kind of a conquering feeling of forcing the boat to steer itself, leaving us free to look around at things like the trees and the ducks.

Just before entering the Gulf Islands, we looked across the strait to the full western exposure of the U. S. San Juan Islands. I was intrigued by an island near the northwest corner of the group, H-shaped Henry Island, because it looked more remote and set aside from the rest of the bigger and more populated

Henry Island cabin

islands. That memory not only lasted, but years later I bought a property there. The property had a wide-open view of the strait and beyond that, the snow-capped Olympic mountains. During the 30 years I owned the property, I was able to spend nearly half of my time there because part of that time I was retired and before that, I was working only three days a week with an associate dentist working in the office the rest of the time. One of my greatest joys there was building blazing fires in the huge fireplace—which I built myself—to both heat the house and cook over.

Not only that, but the next day we passed another intriguing island, Dick Island, which was covered with a heavy first growth forest and with a stand of madrone trees with their huge, twisted bases bulging up from the rocks in strange formations. Many years later I bought this 22-acre island. It had a small log cabin on a bluff with a 200-degree view of the wide-open Strait of Georgia and the peaks of Vancouver Island. I found a madrone tree there that measured 50 feet in circumference and was said to be the biggest madrone in the North America. When I sold

Dick Island

The giant madrone

the island many years later, the buyer, after flying over it once, offered the full asking price; and when we met, he offered me a key to the cabin, so I've been using it ever since.

Once in the Gulf Islands, the current was mostly with us, especially in the narrows between the islands, where there were flocks of white-winged scoters, pigeon guillemots, and rhinoceros auklets. As we passed, some of them turned their heads toward us as if envious of our superior speed.

One of the narrows ahead was shaped like the neck of a long narrow funnel, and with the current's increasing strength, we seemed to be gaining too much speed. Ahead we saw the water dropping like a river and we held on tightly and squirted through at over twice our usual ground speed with the land right beside us screaming by. And as we shot out of the narrows, a shiny white ferry—one of 35 that travel 25 routes throughout this part of British Columbia—was right in front of us. We jerked the tiller hard to port and watched the ferry pass almost next to us.

Some of the islands we passed showed us their madrone trees (called Arbutus in Canada) clinging defiantly to the cracks of the rock banks, with their energy so devoted to gripping the rock that little remained to form bark, so their orange trunks peeled in paper-thin layers, exposing their green inner guts.

At the far end of the Gulf Islands, we located a spot on the chart that looked inviting for a stopover—Silva Bay. To get there however, we had to go through False Narrows, and with a name like that and its extensive reefs, we hesitated. We slowed the boat way down, watched the depth sounder closely and collectively held our breath while watching long shallow reefs lumber by—close and on both sides of the boat. But once past that, we saw the fully forested islands surrounding this quiet bay, and the three of us agreed that this was the right place for spending the night.

We dropped the hook in the middle of the bay and Dale poured Mary Ann a white wine, me a bourbon, himself a tequila. A group of crows were talking things over in a nearby tree. A flock of black and white western grebes floated by with their necks twisted like cobras. A jet-black cormorant stood alone on top of an old piling with his wings strangely bent out to dry. Some bald eagles coasted by, twisting their white heads back and forth but paying no attention to us. Something like a prehistoric pterodactyl glided overhead, landed in an evergreen tree, and then, feeling out-of-place, the great blue heron soon flew off, his loud croaking clamoring then fading in the distance.

Something strange on the most distant horizon grabbed our attention. Right above the waterline a piece of land seemed to be upside down. And right below that was the same piece of land that was right-side-up, with the treetops of the upside-down part touching the treetops of the right-side-up part. Through the binoculars it looked the same way and before long the upside-down part disappeared. We learned later that it was a mirage—which is an unusual optical illusion, where atmospheric reflection by a layer of hot air distorts or inverts reflections of distant objects.

It was getting dark so I lit the small kerosene lantern we used for an anchor light, hung it in the rigging where other boats could see it and we went below for a late dinner.

Before leaving in the morning, we tried to do an engine repair because over the last couple days it had been faltering. I removed the spark plugs, cleaned their inner guts with a wire brush and replaced them—and the motor ran better.

What we didn't know was that this would be just the beginning of continual motor problems throughout most of the circumnavigation, including once in a stormy ocean when the engine would stop completely, and another time, when lost in blinding fog, we would have to grope under sail to find shelter.

After cleaning the spark plugs, we departed Silva Bay and headed north for what we anticipated as being the highlight of our trip—Desolation Sound.

At a thrilling seven-knot speed, we broad reached obliquely across the widest portion of what's commonly called the Gulf (Strait of Georgia). A problem with this route, however, is that there's a large torpedo range charted right in the middle of it. This apparently means that it's possible that submarines could be firing torpedoes here. Scary! But we saw no sign of any such activity; so, to save time we cut across its Northwest corner. This shortcut, however, does not always work. On a subsequent trip in the same place, a large Canadian Navy ship approached us closely, sternly reprimanded us, then kicked us out of the area immediately.

Once across the Gulf, we changed course and motor-sailed, tacking back and forth against a northwest wind. We found that by doing this with the traveler pulled hard to the windward side, exposing more sail to the wind, it not only seemed to improve our speed but helped stabilize the boat.

At the northwest end of the 18 to 30-mile-wide, 125-mile-long Strait of Georgia, we rounded Sara Point and there we got our first full view of what we'd been waiting for—Desolation Sound. There were heavily forested islands everywhere we looked and behind that, huge, glaciated mountains covered the entire eastern horizon. Between these steep-sided mountains are deep fjord inlets, cut by the immense retreat of the ice that once covered this entire part of the continent. Why Captain Vancouver named this Desolation Sound, I'll never know. I found it so breathtaking, I wondered why I wanted to sail any farther.

Our first stop in Desolation Sound was at Refuge Cove. Even though it's in the heart of the sound, it's tucked into the side of a dinky bay and can't be seen until it's right in front of you. Remember the old Popeye movie with Robin Williams?

Refuge Cove is like a small version of that Popeye Village. We docked at its long wharf, bought a few things in its small store, and strolled around looking for Popeye.

We wanted to call Mary Ann's sister to see if she could continue babysitting her kids a little longer so that she could spend for a few more days aboard, however there was no phone there, so along our route the next morning we stopped at nearby Cortes Bay where we did find a phone. Her sister agreed to babysit longer. Seeing our smiles when walking back to the boat, Dale cheered.

I couldn't reach my kids.

Then we sailed to what is considered the gem of Desolation Sound—because of its many arms and coves, almost all wooded and in total protection—Prideaux Haven. Its innermost extension, Melanie Cove, looked especially inviting. Once inside the cove, there were so many beautiful choices for anchoring we couldn't decide which one to take. We chose a niche with a view of the entire cove; and once anchored, Mary Ann and I dinghied ashore. We tied a stern line to a tree to keep the boat from swinging onto the shores on either side and I helped her climb over some slippery rocks, through some brush and onto the top of a small hill. There, like high school kids, we carved, Norm + Mary Ann through the thin outer skin and deeper bark of a madrone.

The water in the cove felt surprising warm so we waded and splashed around. The reason the water is so warm here is because there's little tidal circulation in this whole maze of islands and that's because it's right between the flooding and ebbing currents of Johnstone Strait to the north and the Strait of Georgia to the south.

Because of the warmer water, it's also a perfect place for oysters. So, after the tide was farther out, we picked up a bunch of them where they were growing thick on the rocky beaches. Back on the boat we shucked them and while Mary Ann was frying them, we were all smiling. And if the oysters weren't enough, the crab pot had three big ones in it—which we boiled and also had for dinner.

Did we always eat this well on my boat trips? No. In fact, there were times when we were stuck in places and so low on groceries, it came down to a hunk of old bread and some molding cheese. And there were other places when we were so low on stove fuel that we had to cook ashore over a campfire.

Eating oysters like this, as we did day after day, should we have been worried about red tide? That's when the water turns red from toxic microorganisms. I've even seen this, where large areas of the sea were a brilliant crimson. Then you know not to eat the shellfish—but what about after the red water is gone and the shellfish might still be toxic? Red tide warnings are now available by phone, but they weren't available at the time of our trip. An old rule of thumb for this is to not eat oysters during the months that don't have the letter R in them; and that's because red tide only occurs during those late spring and summer months—but that rule didn't help us because it was June. Even though red tide is said to be poisonous, I've never heard of anyone actually getting sick from it. In fact, growing up, our family gathered and ate shellfish all the time and we never had a problem. On our trip, we hadn't so far seen any red tide, so we kept eating them. Furthermore, at a missionary camp where we stopped at later in the trip, when asking the people there about this, they said that even with red tide God lets them eat anything.

At the end of this great day the three of us just sat quietly in the cockpit after dinner. It started to rain so we rigged a tarp over the boom and began to talk. With the rough weather of the last couple of days, I'd been too busy to think much about my dental office burnout. But now I decided to broach the subject with Dale and Mary Ann. I started by asking them how they liked their jobs. Dale, the quiet, unassuming type, said that as a rocket engineer he was always busy trying to figure things out, but the job itself was okay. Mary Ann, as manager of a restaurant-club, said that she was usually busy dealing with employees and doing desk work, but her job was fine too.

"Well, you two are lucky," I said. "Because I don't like big parts of my job. Filling teeth is fine but it's the stress of managing the business that drives me nuts."

In her soft way, Mary Ann asked, "Then why don't you get rid of that part of the job and have someone else do it?"

"I wish I could, but it's my office and doing that stuff seems like a package deal."

"It doesn't have to be," she said. "Why don't you pass that part of it off to one of your employees. And just stick with the teeth."

"But I feel like the office business is part of my responsibility."

"But getting rid of the burnout is also part of your responsibility," Dale said.

"Norm…" Mary Ann began with that warm southern tone, "when I see you doing something you love like boating, you go into it with a passion." She cleared her throat. "I hope you won't lose any of that passion over this burnout."

"Okay, let me work on it more. I've got over a month left of the trip to think about it and plan for how to do it. Thanks a lot you two."

After that, we just sat quietly in the cockpit and listened to the rain.

Dale, usually unexpressive, finally began talking quietly about some personal things, including the death of his first wife, and then as it was getting late, he dozed, and Mary Ann and I sat closer.

In the morning's light wind, we sailed into Teakerne Arm, tied to a log boom there and dinghied to the base of a huge waterfall at the head of the arm. There we climbed up a cliff to Cassel Lake, which feeds the falls. The shoreline is so steep here that since then, I've let crew members off by backing the boat right into the cliff while they climbed ashore over the transom and later picking them up the same way.

It was in this vicinity that Captain Vancouver anchored for three weeks while exploring the surrounding waterways—and while his crew was brewing spruce beer.

From here we zigzagged north through several scenic channels; and at one particularly rocky narrows we waited for a fishing boat and followed it through, hoping its skipper wasn't perhaps tricking our "all-fun" pleasure boat into a bad spot.

Even though it was getting late, the early summer days in these latitudes allowed us enough daylight to make one last irresistible stop—at the Octopus Islands. To get there however, we had to maneuver the boat between trees that were overhanging both sides of a tiny slit. Then things suddenly opened, and we were inside the island group. The many low surrounding islands were completely wooded, and except for some eagles chortling now and then, there was complete silence. There were niches here and there just big enough for a boat to anchor, so we picked one and after anchoring, went ashore for a warm tide-pool bath.

To bathe on the trip, we sometimes found tide pools like this or freshwater lakes. Other times we boiled a pot of seawater and took it into the boat's head for a steam bath. And as a last resort, we stood on the deck and poured buckets of cold saltwater over our heads. All of this had to be done because the boat's water tank held only 21 gallons and that had to be saved for drinking and cooking.

Before anchoring in a tight place like this, I had learned the hard way to first circle the area where we wanted to anchor looking for rocks. This system doesn't always work however, because once right here in the Octopus Islands years later I bumped a rock and had to work frantically in the dropping tide to get the anchor up and move the boat before it was too late.

There's another thing about anchoring I learned in an even harder way. When weighing anchor without a windlass for leverage, first drive the boat ahead against the taught anchor line to dislodge the anchor. Otherwise, pulling up on the taught line like this can cause gut strain. How do I know? Once after doing this, I noticed a bulge in my gut, which I held in with duct tape for the rest of the trip. It turned out to be a hernia and needed immediate surgery upon my return to Seattle.

It was here in the Octopus Islands where we received our biggest reward for the hardships of the first part of the trip. What we witnessed was right out of the song, "Canadian Sunsets." We watched in awe what turned out to be the most gorgeous, ever-changing and widespread sunset any of us had ever seen. First, the setting sun turned the trees on the opposite shore into a tall picket fence. Then, just as the sun was disappearing behind the horizon there was an instant of bright red flashes radiating upward from the spot where the sun had just set. Lacy clouds above went gray, then ink. The cobalt sky morphed yellow, then rose, and above where the sun had set, it turned a deep orange with white streaks. The sunset finally covered most of the western horizon and its colors folded into horizontal layers all blended together. Later, an immense light rose through the trees on the opposite shore. And that moon turned the land into an eerie night-snow gray and inched its way across the sky.

In the morning we went through Hole in the Wall. It is well-named because it's nothing more than a slit between two steep hillsides. We had to plan for traversing narrows like this at near slack water because otherwise the current in some of them can run downhill at up to 12 knots with rapids like in a raging river. We also had to plan for currents elsewhere in this vicinity, some were violent upwellings and overflows can create vertical walls of water. Our planning paid off and we avoided such encounters.

I had once assumed that slack water in these places occurred at the same time as that of the high and low tides. This, however, is far from true because when it's high tide in a particular place, the water may still be flooding there for hours longer depending on the particular area, and vice versa with the low tides. That's why current tables, in addition to tide tables, are essential for determining the times of the slack water in these places, especially in turbulent passes like those we were now going through.

On our route north we avoided Seymour Narrows, where the current and tide pools can suck large logs under water and spit them up from upwellings—and that's when you don't want to be there.

There was once an even greater danger in Seymour Narrows—Ripple Rock. It was only nine feet below low water, right in the middle of the channel and along the main shipping route to Alaska. Over the years, hitting Ripple Rock accounted for 21 shipwrecks and 114 lives lost. To solve this problem, a shaft was drilled from adjacent Maud Island and below the seabed to Ripple Rock. This took two and a half years to accomplish and cost $3.1 million. Through this shaft, enough explosives to fill 34 railroad boxcars were place under Ripple Rock and at 9:30 a.m. on April 5, 1958, BOOM!—one of the largest non-nuclear explosions in history. 700,000 tons of the top of Ripple Rock were blown up. The event was televised, and as a precaution, the nearby town of Campbell River turned off all public services. That changed the clearance over Ripple Rock from nine to 45 feet.

Next on our route was 68-mile-long Johnstone Strait. Here we faced strong headwinds funneling down this long, narrow, steep-sided strait like it was a giant wind tunnel.

On the inland side of the strait there's a vast myriad of channels, which on the chart looks like an endless spider web. There's one special place here that I had always wanted to see— Butte Inlet. It's shaped like a thin twisted finger extending clear into the ice fields of British Columbia's interior. Second only to nearby Knight Inlet, it's the longest fjord on the coast of British Columbia. It's a 50-mile-long, narrow, deeply cut gorge bounded tightly by towering 9,000-foot mountains. It is said to be one of the most scenic waterways in the world and yet, because of its depth, which drops right off to about 1,000 feet, leaving almost no place to anchor, it is rarely visited. That's why I'd never been able to go there in a sailboat.

Until years later, when once in a powerboat I was able to get to the end of the inlet and back in one day without the need to anchor along the way. While in the inlet we stopped the boat now and then just to crank our heads upward and gawk at the vertical faces and ice-streaked peaks surrounding us. It's the most spectacular mountain scenery I've ever seen from a boat.

At the end of the inlet, we went up the Homathko River, following the deeper outer curves of the flowing river but which was against the flooding current flowing into the inlet. We were met at the Homathko Camp dock by caretakers who offered us lunch, gave us a tour of the place and said that, even though it was mid-August, we were their first visitors of the year.

≈≈≈≈≈≈≈

Another time near here we went too far with this kind of exploration. We wanted to see the entire length of Drury Inlet, right into Tsibass Lagoon at its extreme end. But when we saw a large uncharted rock right in the middle of the lagoon's entrance, we did a sudden 180 and dropped the hook. The two of us then got into the dinghy, and when immediately beyond the large rock, we saw the worst rapids we'd ever seen that close. We tried to turn back, but it was too late. Even at full throttle, the flooding current swept us backwards into the rapids. All we could do was dive to the floorboards while cresting waves broke over the boat and nearly flipped us. For the next several hours we were trapped in the lagoon until the next current change—but thankful we hadn't tried it in the sailboat.

≈≈≈≈≈≈≈

The wind in the Johnstone Strait was causing a bad enough chop that it made our boat act something like a submarine. Because of the roughness we took a rest stop in a notch along the side of the strait which gave us some temporary protection from the roughness. There was another reason for the stop. We wanted to take the dinghy aboard to prevent it from getting away. With the dinghy now aboard, it would always be there, in a situation where we needed it—like to abandon a sinking boat.

We would realize later that a hard dinghy like ours isn't as seaworthy as an inflatable, so on subsequent trips, we took an inflatable, which is also lighter and easier to get aboard. A drawback to inflatables, however, is that when towed, they can do some strange things. Once in a sudden squall ours was lifted airborne, flew upside down and shook the oars loose.

In another notch along the strait, we spotted several large dark objects through the cresting spray. They seemed to be moving but were much larger than any ducks and they seemed to have strange wing-like upward extensions. Perplexed, we headed toward them and finally saw that they were non-other-than killer whales. A pod of over a dozen were rolling and paying no attention to us so we slowed the boat way down and for some time just gazed at them.

Finally, weather-beaten, we arrived at our destination—Kelsey Bay. The whole place turned out to be little more than a ferry dock beside a large breakwater protecting a boat dock. We made a tight, bouncy entrance into the boat dock, but it was full of fishing boats—so with little time or room to maneuver we made a sudden rafting to one of them.

A big surge pinned us against the metal fish boat we were rafted to, jerking and tossing us against it all night. Twice our fenders squirted out with a loud burst that woke us. I went above, forced the boats apart with my feet and jammed the fenders back into place. Early in the morning we were awakened by a loud snap. Our bow line had parted and was torn to shreds, so we acted quickly in replacing it before the boat came completely loose. I also saw that the side of our boat was black and filthy from where the fish boat's tire fenders had been battering us all night.

Later in the morning I phoned my next crewmen, who were to arrive that day by commercial flight. Because of an airline strike however, their flight was canceled. Instead, they arranged for a charter floatplane the next day that would fly them directly to our marina.

To celebrate our extra day, the three of us walked a mile up the road to a town that was mapped as Sayward, but which turned out to be nothing more than a few old buildings including a pub. As we walked into the pub, a man not accustomed to seeing a woman as attractive as Mary Ann here, dropped his drink and blurted, "Oh my God!"

The next morning the three of us watched as a distant speck became a seaplane. After a little twist toward the bay, it landed, taxied through the narrow dock entrance and came right to out boat. The plane dropped off my next two crewmen, Phil and Lloyd, and loaded Dale and Mary Ann aboard. While Phil and Lloyd were unpacking below, I sat in the cockpit watching the plane depart and waving. It became another distant speck and disappeared.

CHAPTER FIVE

BAR FIGHT

*P*hil was a close friend and a neighbor. He and Lloyd were brothers-in-law and Lloyd would later become my partner on other sailboats. As neighbors, Phil and his wife once came by our house after dark playing a loud recording of owls hooting and when we opened the door to see what it was, there they were laughing. I once showed Phil, a veterinarian, how to do a dental root canal on a dog's tooth. Because the dog was strapped to a table, unconscious, with its mouth propped wide open, the root canal was much easier than on a wiggly person in a dental chair.

It was still early in the day, we had plenty of time and they suggested going to Port Harvey, about 15 miles ahead. We received the first clear VHF weather report we'd heard in days. "Northwest wind 10-15 knots..." Even though that would be on our nose, it was good news that it was no stronger.

Going up the rest of long and precipitous Johnstone Strait from Kelsey Bay felt like traveling through a tube with its top torn off. Because of the mountainous terrain, there was no road over this entire 75-mile stretch between the towns of Kelsey Bay and Port Hardy. It was also along this route that Captain Vancouver first felt ocean swells coming from the north, proving that Vancouver Island was in fact an island.

After turning into Port Harvey, we dropped the hook in the first protected niche we found and while I dug clams ashore,

Phil and Lloyd hung Playboy's *Miss July* pinup on the bulkhead as a surprise for me. We had a couple before-dinner drinks, and I enjoyed their enthusiasm over their first day aboard—and I enjoyed the pinup.

In the morning we wound our way through the tiny islands in Havannah Channel, and with a bow watch and an eye on a range behind us, squeezed between the rocks in even narrower Chatham Channel. For a break from this tight navigation, we ducked into Cutter Cove and dropped the hook for a while. Behind the wreck of an old cabin there, I walked the vestige of a trail into a virgin forest that gave the feel of a giant cathedral. It struck me silent, and I just stood there for a while.

After zigzagging through some other twisted passages to our west, we anchored in a small steep-sided bay in Crease Island and sat there listening to our voices echoing back from the shore. Three full degrees of latitude north of Seattle, there was enough light to be able to read from the foredeck until 11:00 p.m.

Underway in the morning, my mind drifted back to my burnout.

"Hey Phil, I want to ask you something about your job as a vet. How much business turmoil do you have in your practice?"

"Why do you ask?"

"Because I've got too much of it and I'm trying to figure out how to get rid of it."

"Well, I don't have a lot of those problems because I keep out of the business part of the practice."

"But how can you do that when it's your business?"

"I just let the staff handle it, and I try to stay out of their way."

"Me too," Lloyd said. "I try to do the same thing in my business."

"I know you guys are right," I mused. "In fact, the last crew told me the same thing. So I've just got to work on it."

At the Echo Bay store there was a radiotelephone that could be used for long distance calls. I didn't get my kids, but I did get Mary Ann. But with Phil, Lloyd, the storekeeper, and a customer all listening to the blaring conversation, I couldn't get too personal. Then my allotted phone time was used up, so I had to say a sudden goodbye.

After anchoring in Claydon Bay, I went ashore to burn the garbage. But in the heavy rain, it wouldn't burn, so with Phil and Lloyd watching through the window, I had to pack it all up and bring it back to the boat. Seeing my anger about this, they passed me an immediate drink. After that and a crab appetizer, I couldn't have cared less about the garbage. It could keep till better weather.

Before heading out into open Queen Charlotte Strait in the morning, Phil fixed himself a Bloody Mary. He claimed that it wards off seasickness. I thought that was ridiculous, but in talking to some fishermen later, they said that this does indeed work, but that any more than one drink can be deadly.

When entering the open strait, we encountered a heavy chop with steep breaking waves—and the motor stopped dead. Even with the headwind badly shaking and pitching the boat, I had to go below and try to repair the motor. The access opening to the motor was so restricted I couldn't reach through it well enough to do the repair. So, mad as hell, I grabbed a saw and cut off pieces of the wood boat paneling to enlarge the opening. As I cut off the pieces I threw them overboard through the hatchway. Knowing how mad I was, Phil and Lloyd, standing there in the cockpit trying to sail the boat, didn't say a word. They just ducked the flying pieces. I cleaned the fuel pump and sucked junk from the fuel line, but the motor didn't start.

After beating into the storm, we arrived at Port Hardy just before dark, tied to the first dock we could find, even though it was dilapidated and the water there was shallow. We awoke in the morning because the motion of the boat had stopped. It was aground. In thick mud, Lloyd waded ashore carrying the anchor. After tying its line to a halyard, we tried to wench the boat onto enough of a heal to float it. It didn't work.

After the next high tide re-floated her, we had a local shop mechanic repair the motor. He said that the roughness must have shaken some dirt loose from the fuel tank and he replaced our fuel filter with a larger one which he said should solve the problem and the motor ran fine. Unfortunately, however, this did not solve the problem, and worse, the subsequent breakdowns happened in places where there would be no mechanic.

The several days Phil and Lloyd were aboard seemed to go fast, but it was time for them to get back to work—and I would then be alone a few days. I moved the boat to a better dock and started thinking again about my burnout. The good news is that I'd been so busy with boating stuff I'd pretty much forgotten about the burnout. So now that I was alone at a dock I was able to sit back and take a fresh look at it.

The underlying problem had to be the stress, and it takes two things to cause stress: an outside cause and a receptive host. So, I decided to try not to allow the outside stressors to bother me. I came up with this idea. Instead of scurrying around the office trying to handle staff things, how about closing the operatory door and allowing no interruptions, leaving me, the patient and the dental assistant alone in the isolated cubicle and letting the office people handle the other business.

In fact, why couldn't my receptionist become my business manager and handle all the office business as well as the staff supervision. Then instead of me having to be the S O B, she would be.

A highly quality staff would help here. Next time someone leaves, why not replace them with the best person I can find and pay them well? Why not also hire an additional employee or two to make things easier for everyone? What's the difference if this increases my overhead, as long as my bottom line is okay for the amount of time I'm working?

A study club I was in came to mind. It was a group of thirteen local dentists who each month visited one member's office, and that was followed by a long evening meeting where we took turns telling the recipient about his run-down office, jammed quarters, overbooking patients, getting behind schedule, inefficient treatment methods, lost income potential, poor staff performance and inadequate time off from work. This rigorous peer review revealed what we couldn't have known otherwise. In my case they told me my office was overcrowded, I was booking patients too tightly and running too far behind schedule. I wondered if improving those things could also help with my burnout problem.

A drunken fisherman at the dock cussed me out for "Flying the American flag in Canadian waters." Seeing this, the fishermen on one of the boats I was rafted to invited me aboard for drinks. One of them started playing a guitar and we all sang songs like "Take the Ribbon from your Hair." After a while we all went up to the pub and one of them, Art, a tall muscular guy, moved in on an attractive young woman with big wondering eyes who was sitting alone at another table. As it turned out she was the girlfriend of the local thug, Kenny, who then proceeded to clobber Art from behind. When Art came back to our table with his face bleeding, the other two guys with me confronted Kenny and a violent scene erupted. Chairs flew. A light fixture was shattered. Loud yelling. All of them streamed out the back door, shoving and slugging. I ran out the door just in time to see Kenny's gang holding off a gathering crowd while he was mercilessly kicking Art in the head with his metal-toed boots. Kenny and his gang disappeared leaving Art lying unconscious, blood and dirt covering his caved-in face.

He was taken to the hospital. I gathered some witnesses' names, testified to the Mounties, and after returning to the boat, jammed the hatch tightly closed. I later learned that Art was recovering from multiple facial fractures. And Kenny had skipped town.

A week later in another town, after thinking that a small pub there looked safe, my next crewmate and I stopped for a beer. A logger the size of a tree trunk came to our table glaring and shinnied up the table's center support post while yelling defiant profanities. The bartender shouted at him to get out of the pub. The logger climbed down, faced the bartender across our table and yelled, "No!"

The bartender yelled, "Get out now!"

The logger yelled back, "I'll leave but I'll be back, and I'll kill you."

We quickly finished our beer and returned to the boat.

Later yet with different crewmen, we were sitting in another pub when a woman flopped drunk into our laps. We eased her onto a table and got out of the pub as fast as we could.

After all that I told my next crews in absolute seriousness that the greatest danger of the trip was not at sea—but in the pubs.

The morning after the fight I cautiously got off the boat and tried to call my kids and Mary Ann. I couldn't reach the kids, but I did get Mary Ann. After telling her about the bar fight, I asked her if she could visit me in Seattle when I returned from the boat trip. She said she'd try.

On the dreary walk back to the boat in heavy rain I walked past the blood patches still there in the dirt, glad that that was behind me.

I needed to get out of this desolate place. I headed the boat back south to the nearest town, Port McNeill. Along the way the sun came out and the town had a friendlier feel than Port

Hardy. At the dock a couple strolling by the boat stopped to talk and invited me for dinner. He was a local doctor and before dinner he received an emergency call about a man who had fractured a finger. In his small powerboat we took the patient to the nearest hospital which was in Alert Bay. While the doctor was treating the patient, I walked around and found what was the largest concentration of totems on Vancouver Island. One with multicolored outstretched wings, is the largest totem in the world—173 feet tall. Finally, we returned to the couple's home for a very late but fun dinner. We talked about how different our two practices were, his in this remote village and mine near downtown Seattle, and although we agreed we wouldn't trade places, part of me wanted this remote kind of life.

Returning to Port Hardy in the morning, several large sleek dolphins circled the boat for some time, seeming to be checking me out. I talked to them, but they didn't answer.

Back in town I met my next crewman, Herb, a new dentist friend. Even as a one-leg amputee, he had recently crossed the Pacific alone in his 36-foot sailboat. The first thing we did was to study the small-scale chart of Vancouver Island taped to the cabin ceiling, the only place on the boat large enough for the chart. Then, after telling him about the bar fight, we got right into his unusual sailing experience.

"Great to have you aboard, Herb. Tell me more about your ocean voyage."

"Yes, it was a long trip, and not that long ago. Our 13-year-old daughter died of leukemia, and my wife and I decided to do this to focus our attention on something else. So, we studied up on boating, bought a sailboat and took off."

"I didn't know about your loss, Herb. I'm so terribly sorry."

"On the ocean you have plenty of other things to think about."

"You said you sailed back alone. Why alone?"

"My wife and I had problems along the way. When it was time to return, we decided to split." After pausing, he continued. "It's just as well. Things weren't working out well between us and being together on a small boat for such a long trip brought that out even more."

"But weren't you worried about sailing back all that distance alone?"

"Yes, but I decided that it would be okay."

"Did you think about asking someone else to sail back with you?"

"Yes, but I didn't know anybody there and I was afraid that taking someone I didn't know could turn out to be a problem, and then what would I do in the middle of an ocean. So, I decided to do it alone. And it worked out okay."

"Even though you had one prosthetic leg?"

"Yes, I was used to that, I got around fine, and it turned out to be not that much of a problem. When I lost my leg I was determined to not let that slow me down. So, I continued to snow ski and water ski, which I'd always done before."

"Damn Herb, you're amazing," I said, and paused. Then I said, "Can I ask how you lost your leg?"

"It was in college. I had a summer job at a cement plant. I was inside of a cement mixer cleaning it out and someone accidentally turned it on, and the blades tore that leg apart."

He was right about his leg not being a problem. It never was the whole time he was aboard. And that would be longer than any of my other crewmen—three weeks. It was great to have him aboard and to learn from his experience.

"Something else, Norm—so you won't feel too sorry for me. I've got a new girlfriend. Her name is Peggy, and things are going well between us."

Herb with his prosthetic leg

"That's great Herb. And guess what. We're both in the same boat, in more ways than one. I too have a new girlfriend."

"You don't say."

"Her name is Mary Ann. She was on the first part of this trip and things went well."

The motor went out again and a strong ebb was sucking us relentlessly into Nahwatti Bar. An equally strong wind was colliding with the ebb and blowing huge breakers over the entire bar. One of the biggest waves twisted the boat abeam, rolled her upside down and dropped her from its crest into the seething fury below. I swam for the surface and my hand hitting the bulkhead woke me from the nightmare, panting but relieved.

I'd been worried about the infamous Nahwatti Bar for some time. It's considered one of the worst obstacles of a Vancouver Island circumnavigation. It's an underwater cliff which, and as in my nightmare, often causes steep waves to break clear across the bar.

CHAPTER SIX

ROUNDING THE HORN

In the morning robins greeted us with loud singing and then we took off. I pumped half a pot of water into the coffee pot, threw in some coffee, and after it boiled awhile, poured myself a cup. Then I removed the grounds, refilled the pot, and put it back on the burner for Herb.

"Damn, this tastes good, Herb. It's the best part of the morning. I don't see how you can stand that weak stuff."

"I guess I've just gotten used to it. And that way I get to drink more of it."

"To each their own."

As the morning warmed heading up Goletas Channel, we put a fishing line over the stern. A solid jerk caused the line to zing. But instead of a fish, a big auklet duck was thrashing against the line. When we unhooked him, he quacked a quick thank you and flew off frantically.

On a subsequent trip here in Goletas Channel, we were traveling at night and the sky ahead began to brighten. The northern lights. As we traveled northward they grew brighter and more widespread, filling over half the sky and continually flashing and sweeping like wide searchlights. Even into the wee hours none of us could bring ourselves to leave the cockpit and stop gawking at them. They were by far the best display of northern lights any of us had ever seen.

At Bull Harbor, the usual stopping point before rounding Cape Scott, the weather was good and Nahwatti Bar looked calm, so we decided to keep going and get that behind us. This meant however that we'd have to go clear around the cape and probably travel 58 miles to the next safe harbor—Winter Harbor.

Right after crossing the bar, the motor stopped, again. We had just gone through a kelp patch, and I suspected the kelp had fouled the prop. Instead, we found that the motor was overheated. We detached the water hose and saw that no water was getting to the motor. So, we checked the thru-hull fitting. It was completely clogged with kelp. As we were cleaning it out, water began gushing into the boat from the opening, so we frantically finished the cleaning and closed the valve. Once the motor cooled, it started right up, and we kept going.

As we rounded Cape Scott with the Scott Islands to our starboard we could barely make out the outermost island, Triangle Island, 28 miles away. It has British Columbia's largest seabird colonies with record numbers of tufted puffins and Cassin's auklets. It also has some of the worst weather on the

Triangle Island

coast, and being totally exposed, even the fish boats rarely venture there. In the early 1900s a lighthouse was built on the island, and even though it was heavily braced and cabled down, in a storm not long thereafter, it blew over a cliff.

Still, I couldn't resist the idea. So, years later I obtained a permit required to visit the island, and on my next circumnavigation the forecast was for a weak front with wind only 15 knots, so my brother and I decided to venture out and give it a try. Along the way we passed a small rock island with about 200 squirming sea lions, all crowded against each other to keep from tumbling into the water below. By noon, with only nine miles to go, the sun was out, but even though clouds were building to the west, we took our chances. We anchored in the NE bight of the island and went ashore, to what felt like being on another planet. While walking over whale bones here and there, we watched thousands of seabirds fly over us before perching on the cliffs. Because there are no trees on the island, the birds are forced to nest on the bare notches in the cliffs, but they'd apparently become use to it and didn't seem to mind. In order to make the next safe anchorage before dark, we quickly returned to the boat and departed. The predicted front never materialized, the west clouds dispersed, the wind was light, and the sun was out all afternoon. We arrived at Sea Otter Cove before dark and just looked at each other in disbelief. In my nearly 50 years of sailing these waters, this was the most adventuresome thing I've ever done, and I've never heard of anyone else doing it.

Did we ever go farther north? Once we made a try for the distant Queen Charlotte Islands. We got far enough north, but the weather was too bad to make the exposed crossing to the islands, so we gave up. On our way back we stopped at the town of Ocean Falls, and what a surprise that was. Because of the recent pulp mill closure there, it had become a modern ghost town, with a six-story building, a large pulp mill and streets full of houses, all empty.

After rounding Cape Scott, Herb and I headed south for the first time and with the wide-open Pacific Ocean to our starboard. This West Coast was the part of the voyage I was most looking forward to. However, because of the vast number of ships that have crashed ashore here over the years, it is called "The Graveyard of the Pacific."

I thought here in open water would be a good place to try the sextant. Especially with Herb's help, because he had used one in crossing the Pacific. A sextant is a celestial navigation instrument used to determine one's location on the open ocean where there's no land in sight. The sextant does this by measuring the angle between the sun, moon or stars and the horizon at any particular time of day. These were the days before GPS when at sea a sextant would be needed. After taking a sun sight, I went below, and it took so long trying to figure it out with Bowditch's three-inch thick navigation book that I started getting seasick and gave up. Herb was too busy steering to help me. There were other times on the trip when we had better luck with the sextant, but I was glad we weren't dependent on it.

In trying to find a place get off the ocean for the night, Sea Otter Cove looked too rocky, and San Josef Bay looked too open to the ocean, so we kept going. To save on fuel, we sailed when we could, but only if we could make about five knots, because going any slower could mean getting stuck overnight at sea, in who knows what kind of weather. In fact, we heard on the radio that the day before a fish boat had sunk here in a storm.

Norm's law says that half of the time there isn't enough wind to sail, and when there is enough, half of that time it's on your nose, so that leaves only a fourth of the time for fair-wind sailing. Luckily we were sailing under full sail in this northwest wind, and we were able to make reasonable speed.

Just ahead it looked like fog—much thicker than we were used to—and we were soon in it. This sea fog isn't like land fog which usually dissipates during the day as the land heats.

Ocean fog

During the summer, the surface of the ocean offshore is warmer, and when the typical onshore wind blows that warmer air over the colder shoreline waters, it forms fog. And this kind of fog can last all day, or longer.

In the entrance to Quatsino Sound the fog thinned and we began to see what looked like vague gray monsters, which turned out to be bulging prominences of land. Then, like ghosts coming out of the fog, suddenly there were fishing boats clustered all around us. We slowed way down because it was difficult to figure out which of their nets went with which boats. After we got past the fishing boats, a large area of white froth appeared right in front of us. It turned out to be a thick foam streak.

We arrived at Winter Harbour just before dark and after all this stuff and a very long day, we crashed for the night.

Headed into the main part of the sound in the morning, I said to Herb, "Well, here we are, Quatsino Sound."

"And look at the chart Norm. It's huge."

"It's the biggest sound on the west coast of the island. Look at these three long inlets."

"Great, that should keep us busy for a while."

"One problem though. These narrows connect them. Quatsino Narrows. I've read that Quatsino Narrows has the strongest current on the whole coast."

After first checking out Neroutsos Inlet, we had to wait till near slack current in the narrows before continuing. Then we nosed into Rupert Inlet, but when we saw a large copper mine at its end, we turned right around. After all that exploring, secluded little Varney Bay felt just right for the night, so we dropped the hook and for hours, watched a black bear noisily chewing muscles almost beside where the boat had swung.

With the thrushes singing and the kingfishers chattering, I rowed the dinghy into the bay's long narrowing inlet and into a box canyon with spectacular overhanging cliffs and caves. I often dinghied into little places like this on the voyage. Places you couldn't get to in the main boat, and where you could feel closer to nature, even though they were sometimes scary.

≈≈≈≈≈≈≈

Over the years, I had become very used to dinghies, and had gained great respect for their use. Once at Shilshole Bay marina in Seattle where I kept my sailboat, a dock mate saw me readying my dinghy on a snowy winter night and said, "You're not leaving now are you?"

When I said, "Yeah," he said, "You're crazy!"

I had been dinghying back and forth this way between work and my rented home on Bainbridge Island on a regular basis. Sometimes the trips were fast and smooth, often with either full sunrises or sunsets, and I got a close look at the ducks. Other times it was rough and capping so that I couldn't plane. Sometimes it was foggy, and I had to steer by a bouncing compass held in one hand and honking a handheld boat horn with the other hand and also trying to hold up a pie tin as a radar reflector to try to prevent ships from hitting me. The winter commutes were usually in darkness, so I used a flashlight to look out for logs.

Dressed warm before leaving that evening, I harnessed myself into the dinghy with a heavy strap, brushed off the fresh snow and started planing across the Puget Sound. With it snowing harder, I could barely see the hand compass and had to guesstimate my course by the direction of the oncoming waves.

When the house lights on the Bainbridge shoreline suddenly appeared, I jerked the boat hard to starboard to keep from hitting the shore. With an arm above my eyes to deflect most of the snow, I followed the shoreline as best I could. Some huge flashes of lightening lit up the sky and I wondered how vulnerable I was to being struck here in open water. A dim flashing light appeared through the snow, which had to be Point Monroe, so I turned west. And after later turning south into what I hoped was Agate Pass, the traffic lights on the bridge lights appeared and I knew I would soon be home.

What an adventure—if you're crazy.

≈≈≈≈≈≈≈

With little wind in the morning, we motored all the way to the end of 25-mile-long Holbert Inlet. Along the way I brought up my burnout issue.

"Herb, I want to ask you something about running a dental office. Frankly, I'm getting burned out. Treating the teeth is fine but the business side of it is driving me nuts. I talked to the last crews about it, and they've convinced me that I need to get rid of that business stuff and turn it over to the staff. But how do I do that when I've been doing it all these years?"

"Norm, I'll bet that as the patients are leaving you're out there at the front desk trying to arrange their next appointments."

"Sure."

"Don't do that."

"Uh…"

"That's what I used to do. But then I started organizing patients' appointments ahead of time and let the secretary make the appointments without my being in on it. Now they determine the length, number and times of appointments."

"I know you're right. Herb, but it's so hard to let go."

"I'll bet you do other things that way too. Like trying to figure out which patients to see next and when. Let the staff do all that and go have a cup of coffee."

"Okay dammit. I'm going to train the staff to do these things. I'll tell them my doctor prescribed more coffee breaks."

I raised a cup to toast him.

On the way out of Holberg Inlet, we stopped at Cole Harbor. From the only phone booth in town, I was able for the first time since leaving on the trip, to reach my kids. I was terribly relieved to hear them sounding okay. Chris and Sheri even asked me how the boat trip was going.

Coal Harbor was named because of a coal mine there, but that was unsuccessful and sometime later it became a whaling center—one of the busiest on the coast until 1967 when the whaling business slowed down. The town didn't have a liquor store, and we didn't have enough to make it to the next town. Next to fuel, booze was the main priority. Without groceries we could always live from the sea and the shores. The nearest town was Port Hardy, on the other side of the island. However, because Quatsino Sound nearly bisects Vancouver Island, Port Hardy is only ten miles away by road. So, I hitched a ride there, and traveling at 45 miles per hour seemed frightening after going five to six knots for the last few weeks. The guy I hitched a ride with did a couple errands and insisted on driving me back to Coal Harbor.

Because of this closeness between Port Hardy and Coal Harbor, boaters wanting to circumnavigate the island sometimes cheat here and trailer their boats across the island. This way they avoid two of the biggest obstacles in a full circumnavigation—Nahwaii Bar and Cape Scott.

Departing Coal Harbor, we were sucked through Quatsino Narrows with a strong ebb current and anchored for the night in a place where we could see the ocean but weren't exposed to it. We couldn't help but worrying about tomorrow's planned rounding of the infamous "Cape of Storms."

CHAPTER SEVEN

CAPE OF STORMS

A head of us now was the most desolate 60 miles of coastline in all of British Columbia, possibly in all of North America. It is the same now as it was when Captain Cook first saw it over 200 years ago, without a wisp of smoke, not a tree disturbed and about the only signs of life, the sea lions and birds.

Each morning before departing I made a habit of pumping the bilge. This was not only to keep it dry, but to see how much water was accumulating. Lately, there was more than usual and other than some dripping from the water pump, we didn't know why—so we had to consider the possibility of hull damage.

As we departed and it became rougher I couldn't help but look below now and then for water—and then my eyes bulged. There was water on the cabin sole. I found that it was squirting from the engine's water hose where we had recently repaired it. Herb turned off the motor and pumped out the water while I repaired the leaking hose as best I could with duct tape, as quickly as I could, because we were drifting toward a rocky ocean shoreline. While I did the repair, Herb readied the sails, in case we needed them quickly.

It was at times like this that we were thankful to be in a sailboat. In a powerboat, we could have been screwed.

The motor did start, and we got out of there fast.

Did I ever make that change to a powerboat, like most sailors eventually do? Yes, but only for a short time and then right back to a sailboat. Ultimately, however, I did make that final change to a powerboat —but it wasn't until I was 82 years old. And even then, guess where I went? Yup, right back to that glorious West Coast of Vancouver Island. But I did it the way porcupines make love—very carefully.

The weather ahead looked worse and built up to about 25-knot south wind—right on our nose. We motor-sailed close-hauled, with the bow pounding into the big ocean waves. The wind was shrieking. With the beating we were taking, the traveler broke. This left the boom along with the mainsail thrashing uncontrollably. We threw a line around the end of the boom to stop the worst of the thrashing and struggled to get most of the sail down. With another rocky lee shore close, we quickly jury-rigged enough of a repair to limp around Kwakiutl and Lawn Points. After navigating carefully through the sea of rocks in Brooks Bay, we entered Klaskino Inlet and there we found what looked like a big, elevated ball of seaweed. It turned out to be our saving grace, in the form of a seaweed-covered mooring buoy. So we tied to it and finally started to breath normally.

"You believe our rotten luck, Herb? First a plugged thru-hull. Then a water leak. And now a broken traveler."

"Norm, I've been giving all this some thought. Here's what you've got to do when you get home. Have a strainer put over the thru-hull, to keep junk from getting into the water intake. Get a bigger and better fuel filter, to keep the fuel cleaner. Have the fuel line and tank thoroughly cleaned. Have a good mechanic check out the entire motor. And have a good rigger check out the spars and rigging."

"Damn, and I thought I had the boat in good shape before the trip. I guess it takes a good shakedown cruise to find out what's really wrong. And I can't think of a more rigorous shakedown than a Vancouver Island circumnavigation."

"Right, Norm. But the good news is that the boat will then be in great shape for your next trip—like maybe another… circumnavigation?"

"That's the last thing I'm thinking about now. Now I'm thinking about a drink."

"The sooner the better."

As was usual lately, there was no radio reception, but the morning weather looked better, the barometer was up two-thirds of a point and there were some breaks in the clouds. Hoping for the best, we took off.

There it was, right in front of us—massive Cape Cook. Commonly called the cape of storms, because it has the worst weather on the entire west coast of Vancouver Island. That's because this whole peninsula protrudes so far out from the rest of the coastline that the usual coastal winds are compressed here and accelerate.

Sure enough, here's where we encountered our worst sea conditions—a combination of strong headwinds, big swells, and bigger ocean waves. We took a shortcut inside of barren and nearly vertically sided Solander Island, trying to stay as close to the island as we dared in order to clear the myriad of rocks just inside. The sea lions and birds on the island watched us passing by, probably wondering what the hell we were doing there. To the other side, the craggy rock walls of Brooks Peninsula rose vertically, and inland from that was a vast alpine wilderness of 2,500-foot-high heavily wooded mountains.

At the far end of the peninsula, we found ourselves in a kelp bed and the sounder read only 30 feet, even though we were far away from land. We slowed way down because this would be the worst possible place to run into a rock. Thankfully the water soon deepened, and we turned into Checleset Bay. After pounding into heavy seas most of the day, we were now, for the first time, able to sail in a fair wind with a sudden burst of speed. Tens of thousands

Solander Island

of sooty shearwaters, murres, auklets, and tufted puffins covered the sea and frantically scurried away from our oncoming boat.

"Well, Herb… we pulled it off—Cape Cook."

"Yeah, glad to have that one behind us."

We checked the chart for a place to spend the night and found some intriguing names, like Battle Bay and Skirmish Islet. With names like that, we figured there might be some evidence of Indian history here. We were not disappointed. Reading in one of our guidebooks, we found that the name Battle Bay came from the history of brutal battles fought here between the powerful and hostile Haidas, who paddled in large ocean-going war canoes, all the way from the Queen Charlotte Islands, to battle the local Checleset tribe here.

With a bow watch and navigating between rocks and islets, we entered the bay and dropped the hook. Ashore we walked to an area charted as "Ind. Vil."

There was an unusual flat grassy area, and sure enough, digging around we found it to be a midden full of old clam shells. Searching through the trees there, we suddenly came face-to-face with a towering, weathered totem. I reached up and touched one of its hands while its six sinister eyes scowled down on me. Searching behind that, we found another totem, this one lying on the sides of its several faces. In the trees behind the totems were

(left and above)
two at Acous Peninsula
(lower photo)
that of a gravesite

old fallen timbers of what had to have been at least one longhouse. The site had what we learned were the three requirements of such a village:

1. Access to fresh water
2. Flat terraces for building longhouses
3. An open view of the water to watch for approaching enemies

In the solitude of the place, we sat and imagined being with the natives having potlatches here beside their campfires.

With a find like this, we explored more by dinghy, to see what else we might find. Looking closely along the tree line of a small island we spotted some deep weather-beaten grooves at the base of the lower limbs of some of the oldest cedars. Going ashore there and breaking through the trees, we couldn't believe what was right in front of us. Some rotting dugouts with bones in them and on top of one of them, three mossy human skulls with their sockets staring right at us. We learned later that this was an Indian burial grounds and that the scar-like grooves in the tree limbs were wear-marks of ropes used to raise canoes with bodies in them.

In the morning we headed south through a narrow passage between some of the outer portions of the wind-swept Bunsby Islands. The passage turned out to be so rocky that even proceeding slowly we hit and grounded on a rock. From the dinghy we quickly set the anchor and were able to kedge off. Then we dropped the hook in a protected bay inside the outermost island of the group and walked the beach. We saw deer and racoons, and after passing through an opening to the ocean side of the island, found a partly decomposed 40-foot whale. I cut away one of its mandible bones. Back at the boat, I scraped off what remaining meat I could and put it in the lazarette inside of a double plastic bag. For the rest of the trip however, whenever we opened the lazarette, there was the stink of that bone.

For the last several days, in over 70 miles of traveling, we had not seen another boat.

CHAPTER EIGHT

INLETS, THREE IN A ROW

Norm was asked, "look at this chart. Now we've got these three major inlets right in a row. This should be one of the best parts of the trip."

"That's just what I've been thinking. And we've got time to explore them all. Look how small his first one is, Kyuquot Sound, compared to that last one that spreads all over the chart. It's the smallest sound on this coast. But it's still got these neat little arms that spread here and there."

"And the next two, Esperanza Inlet and Nootka Sound are connected on the inside. That means we can get off the ocean for a while."

"Yeah, we can use a break."

We also needed fuel before long, and Zeballos and Tahsis were the only towns on this whole stretch of the coast that looked like they might have fuel. Both towns were out of our way, but Tahsis was the closest, so that's where we would later go. Our ice was also low. So low in fact that we'd been wrapping what little we had left in towels so it would keep longer.

On our way to Kyuquot Sound in some sloppy sea conditions, the motor started acting up again. I removed the spark plugs and tasted saltwater on them. I cleaned them, along with the cylinders, as best I could and then disassembled and cleaned some water out of the carburetor. Nothing helped. In fact, the motor was running so badly we decided to stop at some community charted as Kyuquot. To get there however, we were forced to motor-sail through a garden of rocks and some narrow S-shaped passages, all the time with me barking orders to Herb from the bow while he was steering and adjusting sails. Then we limped into the entrance of a hidden cove, which turned out to be Kyuquot. It was a remote wilderness hideaway with a quaint Indian village on one side of the cove and a smaller community on the other side.

We barely made it to the first dock. A fisherman there volunteered to try to fix our motor and while lying twisted on his back, I complained about access to the motor. He simply said, "It's a boat, man." The motor then ran better but he wouldn't take any money.

At a nearby floating fish camp, we got free chipped ice and a hot shower. A fisherman there gave us a three-foot halibut and a smaller salmon that he said were too small for him to sell. With a hose we found lying on another float, we filled the water tank, and bought a few things at the tiniest store I'd seen on the trip. After all this, we just sat there for a while, enjoying the peacefulness of this little place. Years later, when my artist daughter saw it, she said that if she ever disappeared to look for her here.

Entering Kyuquot Sound itself, the fog had rolled in for a while, covering everything but the mountain tops—which we used to steer by. We were now getting so used to fog it was becoming more of a challenge than an apprehension.

We took our time here, first sailing to the end of finger-like Kashutle Inlet and later anchoring for the night inside the surrounding hillsides of tiny Hankin Cove.

In the morning, after eating some crab from the pot, we went into another finger of the sound, Tahsish Inlet. In getting there we passed under an overhanging eagle's nest with its occupants screaming at us for coming so close to their home.

For the night we anchored in narrow Amai Inlet.

Once anchored I took a long walk on a logging road, and for the first time, was able to positively spot a secretive Swainson's thrush. I'd been listening to their beautiful calls for weeks but could never see one. This little guy was perched on a limb beside the road, his throat pulsating out fluteish ascending spirals. My dad had been a local bird authority, so I grew up learning to identify birds. Then—there he was—my long-deceased father, sitting on a stump waiting for me. We talked about the thrush that he had brought to me, the boat trip which he approved of, and Mary Ann who he said he liked. Then he left the stump, and I knelt down beside it, and cried.

Trying to haul anchor in the morning, it was stuck so badly even the two of us couldn't lift it. So, with a winch we hauled it up—along with a sunken log that it had gotten attached to.

After checking out the other inlets in Kyuquot Sound, we rounded Rugged Point through a brilliant red tide, wondering if it had poisoned the shellfish we'd been eating—but we felt fine. Clear Passage was well-named because during the hour we were passing through it, a long group of small reef-like islands protected us from the ocean. Entering Esperanza Inlet, we took a shortcut inside of Catala Island, where we passed several unusually tall and tightly-grouped caves. Dinghying ashore, we found that they were interconnected on their insides so we wandered in and out of as many of them as we could, wondering how many natives might have done this over the centuries.

"Look at this side inlet that's all by itself, Norm, Nuchatliz Inlet. I wonder what it's like."

"Let's find out."

Entering the inlet, we stopped at what was charted as an Indian Reserve. Getting there was a rocky challenge but then it opened up and we dropped the hook beside a tiny village. It was barely protected from the ocean but had a sweeping view of it. Apparently few people visit here because as soon

At Nuchatliz

as we went ashore two little kids ran down from their house and grabbed us. Imagining my own kids doing this, I lifted the little boy by his waist and put him on my shoulders while his sister hung onto my pant legs.

On our beach walk, we grabbed a crab that was scurrying along the shoreline, broke it apart and sat down on a log and ate it raw.

Going farther into the inlet, we peeked through a slit into three-mile-long Inner Basin. The entrance was extremely narrow and looked iffy. There was no current listed for it, but there was an obvious current flowing out; so we figured at worst, we could always drift back out with the current. After dodging a mid-channel rock, the boat barely fit through the slit. The basin was surrounded by tall hillsides, and it gave the feeling of being in a large mountain lake. We dropped the hook and cheered our accomplishment. Looking back at the entrance, the current was flowing stronger and soon became a small waterfall tumbling over the hidden rocks. We were stuck there for the night. But not a bad place to be stuck. In the morning we waited until the current looked slack and made the exit without trouble.

Entering Esperanza Inlet I said to Herb, "Well, where do we go from here?"

"Look at the chart Norm, just ahead through this little bottleneck is Queen Cove. Couldn't be more protected. After squeezing out of that last slit, don't you think we deserve something easier for tonight? You know, Norm, I have to say, I might have sailed across the Pacific, but this stuff is new to me and I'm really enjoying it. "

"So glad you are, Herb. Queen Cove sounds perfect to me too."

Ashore in the cove we checked out another midden, and like the natives must have done here for hundreds of years, we dug and ate some clams for dinner, quietly enjoying the solitude.

In the morning, while exploring two several-mile long fingers of the main inlet, a nearly 75-foot totem appeared out of nowhere. As we slowed to take pictures, a local from one of the indigenous tribes suddenly appeared in on outboard, probably trying to protect the totem, so we kept going.

On our way to Tahsis, we stopped at the small community of Esperanza. It turned out to be a missionary camp. Its leaders, the Johnsons, who had been doing missionary work on the coast for years, showed us around. Later at the boat, they brought us a flower. We placed it right under the Playboy pinup, and coming from missionaries like this, we couldn't bring ourselves to remove that flower for the rest of the voyage, even though it became wilted, sagging and looking as tired as we felt by the time we got back.

From there we gave Mrs. Johnson and two girls from the camp a ride to Tahsis. Wow, a big town for a change. It had one of the largest wood mills in the country, producing two million board-feet of hemlock and spruce lumber per day. I asked a guy there how to pronounce Tahsis and he said to think of "Assis."

After getting fuel we took a walk to town, bought supplies, had a beer in the pub, and played pool with the locals. I tried to phone Mary Ann and the kids but couldn't reach them. Then, even though it was painful, I phoned my lawyer about the divorce proceedings. He said things were gradually progressing, so I relaxed a little.

In moderate headwinds funneling in from the ocean, we motor-sailed down 15-mile-long Tahsis Inlet. It was so narrow in places and the surrounding hillsides so steep that our voices echoed back at us along the way. That inlet led us to Nootka Sound. Exploring around in the upper reaches of the sound, we found a deserted marble quarry in Hisnit Inlet and then anchored for the night in the same part of Bligh Island where Captain Cook's crew cut trees to replace the deteriorating masts on his ship. The next day was the first sunny day we'd had in weeks, so we sat there all day long. We cleaned up the boat, our clothes and ourselves, and then gathered a bucket of clams and oysters for dinner.

Next we visited Friendly Cove, where 200 years before, Chief Maquinna watched Captain Cook make his first North American landing. The cove was then full of longhouses, but now only one family lives there—the Williams. Ray Williams, a descendant of Maquinna, gives us a less-glorious account of Cook's arrival. His ship was so broken down, their people had to tow him in.

This is also the site of the historic Nootka convention where in the 1790s meetings were held between Captain Vancouver, representing England and Captain Quadra, representing Spain. Their meetings were congenial, with lavish feasts, and finally settled, averting a war between the two countries, and giving England rights to these portions of the Pacific Northwest.

The historic sea otter fur trade also started here, beginning with Captain Cook's introduction of these quality furs to much of the world. The unusually soft furs brought an international rush of ships, which put little Friendly Cove on the world map. As a result of over hunting however, the species was brought to near extinction, and just before it was too late, in 1911 a treaty was formed protecting them. In all the time since then, only a small percent have returned. Back at the entrance to Kyuquot Sound, we had seen a group of them gathered on some nearby rocks, casually watching us passing by.

Once anchored in Friendly Cove, we walked along a crooked and partly submersed wharf, with water above our ankles in places. Standing on his porch, Ray watched us approach. Over the years, and many visits since then, we've become friends and I once followed him by boat to Tahsis because he wasn't sure of his broken-down motor. After meeting Ray, we walked a trail surrounded by dense blackberry brush, past a tall totem to a small kind of out-of-place church with two beautiful stained-glass windows commemorating the Nootka convention. Beyond that were two neatly fenced graveyards, one with a large sewing machine belonging to one of the deceased.

With a heavy rope attached to the end of another wharf, we pulled ourselves to a place below the lighthouse where we could jump ashore and climb up a cable track to the lighthouse. Lighthouse keeper, Ed, who'd been working there many years, showed us around. At the light itself, there was a loud generator house with a large tank holding thousands of gallons of fuel that kept its large projector bulb and horn operational. Then we inched our way over a swinging bridge to the helipad used for supplying the lighthouse.

After departing Friendly Cove in fog, we followed a dead reckoning track as best we could and made the long rounding of Estevan Point. Listening to its foghorn slowly passing by, we were careful to stay well outside the twelve-fathom curve because of the many rocks charted just inside that arched rounding. Because the point juts out so far into the ocean, the weather and waves here were worse. Apparently because of the roughness, the motor faltered again. Trying to repair it in the sloppy seas, I became seasick and gave up, so we kept sailing in the light wind.

Our plan after rounding the point was to sail along the next shoreline, and using the sounder, follow that to Hot Springs Cove. In the fog however, we instead came across a buoy identified as the entrance to Hesquiat Harbor. It was the wrong place, but it was getting late, and we needed a place to stop. We had no chart of the harbor, so we had to follow the description in the British Columbia pilot for how to get over the bar. Without seeing land on either side, we passed through a thick kelp patch, hoping it wouldn't run us into the side of Vancouver Island. After crossing the bar, we turned west, and still without seeing land, even at three fathoms, we dropped the hook. Only then and after drifting in, did we see land.

"Well, Herb, we pulled off another one."

"Thank God."

Walking the beach there in the morning we found some large piles of white horse clam shells, from clams that must have been uncovered by storm waves. Using a couple of the biggest shells as shovels, we dug enough of these large clams for dinner.

The next morning, we roamed farther into the harbor. Ashore back in the woods we saw a broken-down shack. We had an uneasy feeling about going ashore and checking it out—and we were glad we didn't. We learned later that a strange old woman known as Cougar Annie lived there and over the many years she was there she reportedly shot over 100 cougars for their bounties and had five husbands, some of whom disappeared... *mysteriously*.

Instead, we stopped at a nearby beach for a walk—and that turned out to be as much of a mistake as Cougar Annie's might have been. A big black bear was headed our way. While frantically untying the dinghy and pushing it off, the bear bounded up almost face-to-face with us.

≈≈≈≈≈≈≈

Black bears are not generally considered dangerous. However, I had had a couple encounters with them that made me wary. Once when camped in the high country of the Olympic Mountains, we were awakened by a black bear going through our packs for food right beside us. We froze in our sleeping bags, and our stirring made the bear retreat, but not very far. While he was closely circling us, we packed up and got out of there so fast we forgot what was left of our food, so we had to hike out for two days eating nothing but the berries we found along the way.

Another time, while working as a ranger in Yellowstone National Park, I had to catch a bear cub who would have died on its own after its dangerous mother had to be shot. When I trapped the cub in a culvert, it turned into a mean little bear and bit me in the leg. I still have the scar.

I also had a scare from a grizzly bear in Yellowstone. We had trapped it and were taking it to a more distant location where he wouldn't be a danger to tourists. With my partner standing by with a gun, I let him out of the trap. But instead of running away, he turned on me and reared up on his hind legs, growling. I banged on the trap with a stick and froze. Finally, he took off, my partner put his gun back in its holster and I started breathing again.

≈≈≈≈≈≈≈

In the light morning wind we sailed for Hot Springs Cove. Along the way we passed some huge beachfront caves with mysterious black interiors. We talked about exploring them but that would have involved anchoring out and landing the dinghy on this exposed ocean shore. And if the weather turned we could have been trapped there. Instead, we opted for continuing, giving us that much more time to soak in those badly needed hot springs.

CHAPTER NINE

HOT SPRINGS SPELL

It had been cold lately and we didn't seem to feel dirty—or even care. Today however, it was warmer. I noticed an oily smell and maybe some gasoline. I sniffed around to determine where it came from. My clothes perhaps? While sniffing, I happened to lift an arm, and had to hold my breath. Herb and I sat farther apart than usual.

"We're getting foul, Herb."

"We really need those hot springs, Norm. I hope they're as hot as we've heard."

"Yeah."

We were also getting weary. Weary from getting lost in fog and then holding our breath entering Hesquiat Harbor without ever seeing land. And from being seasick trying to repair the broken-down motor in the bouncy ocean.

"This damn motor is really getting me down, Herb. You realize so far on the trip it's crapped out four times? That means four times getting seasick trying to repair it. Usually in thick fog. And then groping around without a motor trying to find some kind of protection. And here we are again. This time headed for Hot Springs. And with the damn motor barely limping."

"I know you've had your problems, Norm. I'm glad I wasn't with you all those times,"

While steering, Herb's eyes were searching the shoreline. "I can't find the harbor. Can you see it Norm?"

"No, but it has to be there. I'd keep on this course for a while."

On the chart the harbor was distinct. But even though we were getting close, we couldn't see its entrance. In fact, we were getting so close we were getting worried about some offshore rocks.

On charts things are so obvious, but when you're there on the water, the same things can be so difficult to identify. Climbing the mast would help but what you really need is to become an eagle for a while. And unless you happen to be approaching a bay as narrow as Hot Springs Cove straight on, you can't see it until you're almost there.

Finally, two rocky points began to separate, and between them, a slit opened.

"I guess that's it."

Once inside the cove we looked for houses or docks or hot pools but saw nothing. Ten minutes later, still nothing. Then, around a bend to the right, a weathered dock appeared. A long, tall pier with two attached wharves. Faded red railings identified it as a government dock. At the head of the dock brush was reclaiming a deteriorating building with broken windows. Our official guide, British Columbia Coast Sailing Directions, listed Hot Springs as a community with a store, post office, telephone, diesel and gasoline fuel, and fresh water. None were there. No dock facilities, no residents, no community—no nothing. So how were we to get fuel?

We docked as we'd become used to without a motor. With the mainsail dropped to slow the boat and the jib up for maneuvering, Herb stood on the bow with a mooring line and while steering, I stood in the cockpit with a stern line. Once turned alongside the dock, I released the jib sheet, letting the sail flap in the wind. That slowed the boat enough so we could both jump to the dock with our lines and tie up.

Sometime later a fishing boat docked. Its skipper told us that the dilapidated building used to be the store, but that it had closed a few years ago.

Herb asked him where we could get fuel.

"Ahousat."

We didn't have enough fuel to make it there and we hated to depend on the fickle wind. So, I asked him if he used gas or diesel.

"Diesel."

We of course needed gasoline. Herb and I looked blankly at each other and said nothing.

An hour later another fishing boat approached. We eagerly helped him dock—even though these commercial fishermen never seem to need help docking—and I probably begged more than asked if he used gas.

"Gas."

Trying to control my excitement, I said, "We're almost out and we thought we could get some here. Can we buy a few gallons from you?"

"How ya gonna get it outta my tank?"

"We've got a small bilge pump."

"Never mind, I'll pump it for ya. How much ya need?"

"Just enough to make Ahousat."

After we'd gotten the gasoline, Herb and I sat down, each with a beer and I said, "I know we're tired and filthy but let's try to repair the motor before we go to the springs. Okay, back at Cape Scott, the motor wouldn't run at all. And after we cleaned out the carburetor it ran. Now it starts but it doesn't keep running."

"Right," Herb said. "What could be causing this? Maybe junk in the fuel line."

"Yeah, we've only got this one small filter that I bought back in Port Hardy, and these fishermen have two or three big filters on their engines."

I opened the upper deck hatches to put some light on the engine compartment. Below, I opened the port sliding door—the only access to the motor. And I stared at what I could see of it.

"Okay, you son-of-a-bitch, here I come again… I'm going to whip you yet."

Lying twisted on my side, my nose bent against the motor, one hand squeezed behind the fuel line, I loosened its hose clamp. As I worked I ranted. "One of my main requirements on the next boat will be motor access. How the hell do they expect anyone to repair a motor through a hole the size of this? See where this opening is enlarged, Herb? That's where I cut it open more, before you came aboard. I'd been struggling with a repair and there wasn't even enough room to fit a wrench on the nuts. So, I grabbed the saw and cut parts of the partition away. As I sawed, I ranted and threw the pieces of wood overboard while Phil and Lloyd were above trying to sail the boat and ducking the flying pieces."

Then I asked Herb to crank the motor while I squeezed a plastic cup under the disconnected fuel line. But instead of flowing nicely into the cup, gasoline spurted all over my arm.

"Stop! that's enough!"

After reattaching the fuel line and wiping up the spilled gas, I hollered to him to start the motor again. But after several minutes, it faltered and even though he desperately pumped the throttle, it died.

"Damn!"

"Hey Norm, why don't you detach the fuel line again and see how the gas comes out of it now."

"Good idea."

I repeated the body twisting drill and Herb cranked the motor. This time gas only trickled out of the line.

I shook some mushy material out of the line, and with my mouth to it, sucked out more of the gas-mush mixture and spit it into a bucket. Then I got the hand bilge pump and squeezed its intake hose around the fuel line. Getting some suction this way, I pumped out more of the mush. Finally, the gasoline flowed more freely. Then I removed the fuel filter, washed it in gas, blew several deep breaths into its intake and replaced it. Then the motor ran—and it kept running. Because of our limited fuel however, we couldn't test it for long.

After cleaning up the mess, Herb and I looked at each other, and almost in unison, said, "Let's find those hot springs."

We climbed the steep foot ramp, walked the length of the pier and first nosed inside the vacant store. Some of its floors were tilted, one corner of its roof sagged, and it stunk of mold and garbage.

Scouting for the trail to the springs, we tried working our way through some openings in the brush and beyond one of the openings, we balanced across the solid portions of a broken door and over some wobbly planks.

"This must be it…"

Herb thought the rough path would be too tough for his artificial leg, so he decided to sponge bathe on the boat instead. I reeked of fresh gasoline and old sweat and badly wanted those springs.

"I hope you make it, Norm. See you back at the boat."

The trail was a bizarre and slippery mixture of dilapidated boardwalk, rotting cedar sections and mud. Many of the

Hot springs trail

hand-split cross-slats hung loose, broken, or were missing or reattached askew. I had to watch every step to avoid slipping into mud or jamming a leg between slats. Where slats were missing, I balanced on their support logs, trying to avoid the protruding nails that remained. When I misjudged, some of the nails bit through my thin boat shoes.

Stairs with missing steps and loose or collapsed railings rose or dropped on most steep portions of the trail. At those places I had to either balance with outstretched arms or grab whatever I could find to grab.

At one steep, muddy place, the end of an entire stairway cantilevered free. When I started to walk it, it bounced and twisted like a swinging footbridge. I opted for the mud. At another place, the boardwalk rose up the root of a fallen tree, ending high in midair and I again chose the mud.

In a strange way, the trail had character. I cussed it in places, but smiled in other places, sometimes even shaking my head in amused disbelief.

Ferns and salal grew in strange arrangements from the rotted centers of many of the cedar sections. Green lined both sides of the trail. Green salal, green ferns, green berries, green moss. I ate some of the riper salmon berries and used some of the thick moss for toilet paper. Actually, it was better than toilet paper.

The sides of much of the trail were walls of salal. Salal in inland areas is usually a knee or waist-high shrub. I've cultivated it in the woods around my home because it forms a nice ground cover. In Vancouver Island's coastal rain forests however, it grows to twice a tall man's height and its stems to wrist size. Its branches intertwine so tightly that in places one can hardly push an arm between them or even see the ground through them. At Cape Beale, salal grows so thick that the lighthouse keeper there once told me he was unable to get through it to rescue a fisherman shouting from a nearby rock after his fishing boat crashed onto it.

Now and then I stopped just to gawk at the gigantic cedar trees. Their trunks grow up to eight feet in diameter, although it's difficult to judge just where to measure the diameter of an old cedar because they flare into the ground. Where they flare, sometimes into multiple trunks, I could look through the openings, like looking right through a tree.

Hemlocks grew against some of the cedars like they were strangely mating with each other, with the hemlock foliage seeming to grow from both trees. These parasite hemlocks grow from infants, sucking their life from the perhaps thousand-year-old cedars. Other cedars had succumbed, towering as silver monarchs, refusing to lie down and act dead.

After maybe half an hour, the trail dropped, and I heard the ocean surf roaring and the Sharp Point whistle blaring. Then I smelled something peculiar like sulphur.

After a couple more turns, the trail led to a small bubbling pool. I bent down and tried to put a finger in it. Scalding. The pool's overflow trickled down a streamlet and ended, along with some other streamlets, in a rushing waterfall. The waterfall dropped enough for a person to stand under it and spread wide enough to cover him——but it looked too hot to try. From the falls the water tumbled into a shallow pool, then gurgled through a deep vertical crack in the black rock where it formed a series of three lower pools.

Everything was steaming—the waterfall, the pools, and beyond that, their outlet, flowing right into the pounding ocean surf.

A large log hung suspended across the fissure enclosing the pools. It was too far from the forest to have fallen there. The only way it could have gotten that high, even at high tide, was to have been hurled there by huge storm waves. The flood from such a storm would have to have filled the entire fissure, submersing the pools and obliterated the waterfall. Intrigued by the log, I couldn't resist walking across it—but balancing very carefully.

No one else was there. I peeled the smelly clothes from my smellier body, rinsed them in a pool, and laid them on some rocks to dry. I tried to put a leg into the highest pool. Too hot. I worked my way over the rocks to the middle pool. Still too hot. Beyond that, both sides of the fissure rose vertically. Inching downward, I clutched any irregularities I could grip in the rock walls, with my feet fumbling for the flattest places on the slippery rocks. Using a mountain climbing principle of three-point suspension, I moved only one foot or hand at a time while maintaining firm contact with the other three. I eased into the lowest pool. Just right. I laid my head back on a smooth rock and closed my eyes.

On the voyage, I had been timing the boat's progress to estimate the times of arrivals at various places. But here in the hot springs I never even looked at my watch. I just soaked and soaked and soaked.

One-by-one, I felt the motor problems, the gas shortages, the fog, the seasickness, the getting lost, the storms, the rocks, and even my office burnout all draining away into the ocean below me. My body drooped limp. So, while limp I partly floated, my arms gurgling with the water and my mouth hanging open. I wondered if this is what heaven was like. I wondered if this was real, or if this was all that was real. There, smiling through the steam, were my three kids, and then, Mary Ann. I drifted away.

Sometime later, I became aware of the heat. So aware that I couldn't stand it any longer. I hauled myself out and sat hot in the cool air. When I had cooled some, I slipped back into the pool again. Then I hauled myself in and out—again and again. Finally, I pulled myself up through a crack in the rock wall, to a surface facing the ocean and flopped, in front of the low sun, feeling cleansed from skin to core. Water droplets began forming on my skin, like on a freshly waxed car. I sat watching the surf suck holes out of the shoreline and then plunge them full. As the sun was setting, the colors of the trees, rocks and water darkened, and the sky turned yellow. I sat until I noticed the cold air on my skin.

I looked at the falls again—and wondered if I could now stand the heat. Slowly, I backed into them. The water pounded over my shoulders, back and arms with a powerful massaging vibration. Finally, I flopped aside on a rock, with my muscles shaken limp. I felt drugged as well as euphorically relaxed, like from a tranquilizer, or the way my patients must feel under the gas.

Years later, I went too far with this. The rest of my crew had left the springs earlier, but I stayed and soaked. Fatigued, I finally crawled out of the pool, and because I knew I was late, ran most of the trail back to the boat. The trail was better then, and the running became kind of fun. Back at the boat however, I had some strange sensations that lasted for hours, like I was in a stupor. Since then, I don't soak so long and don't run back.

After returning to the boat, I found Herb roaming the dock. At Hot Springs Cove there's not much else to do. Elsewhere, boaters go ashore to check the community or the beach, but at Hot Springs there's no community, and at high tide, no beach. Instead, the coarse rock and mud beach ends in salal.

Though we were confined to the dock, we didn't feel confined. We talked with some pleasure boaters and fishermen who had docked while I was at the springs. Conversations started with, "How's sailing?" "How's fishing?" "How were the springs?" "Where are you from?" "Where you headed?"

The fishermen across the dock offered us the use of their hot charcoal broiler and their extra corn-on-the-cob.

"Waun, tuh, thre, fuor, fiv, siks, sehvan, ate, nin, tehn," a dugout full of kids yelled in unison, stroking up the cove. They were coming, along with adults cheering from an outboard, from an Indian village farther in the cove. Conversations at the dock stopped and many of us stood and watched. Later, periodic shouting from the village's evening volleyball game interrupted other dock conversations.

"What if a tsunami hit here, Herb. With the earthquakes we have here on the West Coast, what if one of them brought a tsunami right into this little inlet."

"That's ridiculous, Norm. What are the chances of that? That's one thing I'm not going to worry about."

"I know. But I wouldn't want to be here if it did happen."

That in fact is exactly what happened right here in 1964; and along with extensive damage along this coastline, it funneled right into Hot Springs Cove and devastated the entire Indian village. Thankfully, the residents had enough warning to get to higher ground so there were no casualties.

It was getting late, but we just couldn't go to bed yet. It was still daylight, and we didn't want to miss any of the activities at the dock. Heads turned toward an otter that slithered to the surface. It raised its head to swallow a fish and rolled under—again and again and swallowed more fish. People chuckled and kidded about it taking over the limit of fish. Heads turned the other way, watching a mink strolling along the dock, begging for food from the boats. Then there was a sharp piercing whistling and heads twist upward. A pair of eagles circled low, swiveled their white heads back and forth and landed in a tall tree near the dock, occasionally looking down at us. And in the cockpit, we too were perched, occasionally looking up at them. When it became too dark to see them, we finally broke the silence and bid them good night.

We slept late in the morning. Given the charm of the place, we didn't feel like rushing off. I took another trip to the springs. By afternoon more and more fishing boats had arrived and a few pleasure boats. In fact, so many boats that the dock space became full, and they began rafting together, in some places several boats deep; and other boats anchored out. Most of them had come in to wait out a near-gale they reported at sea. In the cove however, it was calm and warm.

At the dock a transformation began to unfold. We stayed for it. A floatplane landed, and because the wharves were full, it taxied to the beach where its passengers waded waist-deep to the shore. Another floatplane landed and with its big propeller roaring, taxied directly to our boat. We grabbed one of its wings and held it in place while its six passengers climbed out, over our boat, and onto the wharf.

From some fishermen docked near us, we traded half a case of beer for a halibut and two buckets of ice. The chipped ice went in our cooler which was getting low again. The small amount of salt added to the ice for icing the fishermen's catches seemed to actually improve the taste of our drinks. Even my Jack Daniels.

Now and then we joined the crewmen of a sailboat with a broken-down motor. While trying to help them solve their motor problems, their faces gradually relaxed and we had drinks together. Later that night, after working with flashlights on parts spread over the wharf, they finished the repair. And with others watching, their motor groaned, belched and started. Everyone cheered.

The crew of another boat invited us aboard, where we visited with their traveling friends—two dogs and a starling in a cage.

Walking by another fishing boat, her skipper said hi. He called himself Jim Clarke. He said his family operated the Hot Springs store until it closed. Jim's father, Ivan, after years of selling goods along the coast by boat, established the Hot Springs store in the 1930s, and in 1954, he donated 40 acres to help establish Maquinna Provincial Park, where the springs are located. Later I would meet Jim's brother, Hugh, who operates the Ahousat store and a third brother, Art, the Tofino wharfmaster.

Across the wharf, the deckhand on a fishing boat dumped a container of garbage over the stern and others at the dock gave him *stern* looks. Cans, bottles, paper, and food scraps drifted around with the current. Von Doit, the lone sailor aboard a crude sailboat appeared with a high-powered rifle. He fired repeatedly at the garbage, and when he sank a bottle or can, others at the dock cheered. Von later showed us some large

Von Doit

boxes of ammunition stowed aboard his boat. He said he had stashes of ammunition, guns, and food along the coast which he planned to use after the worldwide nuclear war.

After that, I squatted beside two kayakers organizing their gear which was spread out on the dock.

"You sure can pack a lot of gear into these little kayaks."

"Yeah, holds about 300 pounds. See how it all fits way up here under the bow and stern."

"How rough a weather can you handle on the ocean?"

"These kinds of kayaks are designed for the sea. They've crossed oceans. We're so low the wind doesn't catch us much."

After that conversation even our small sailboat, with a warm dry cabin, seats, bunks, stove, head, and cooler seemed like a mansion.

A traditional wooden sailboat on the wharf caught my attention. I strolled by and her skipper invited me aboard and introduced himself as Jay Benford.

"Oh, you're the boat designer," I said. "We just saw one of your boats under construction at Coal Harbor. A Benford 40, I think."

"Yes, she's the sister ship of this one."

We couldn't resist periodically strolling by the biggest boat on the wharf. It was an approximately eighty-foot U. S. powerboat. A woman popped out from the cabin to talk and later came by our boat. She complained about their skipper's working everybody aboard cleaning brass and woodwork, and her not getting along with many of the crew. She invited us aboard their boat. Its crew stared at us inhospitably and we spun around and exited as fast as we had entered.

Two outgoing teenage boys hopped aboard our boat and asked for wine. They sucked it down and asked for more, and for cigarettes. We declined. When we later had to leave the boat, for the first time in weeks we locked the hatch.

Then came the highlight of the evening. I was introduced to a woman with gigantic breasts, stepping from a fishing boat.

One of its crew said, "Hi Norm, this is Tits."

"Well, hi, ah…" 1 gulped, "I see why they call you that…"

Others at the dock began to gather, all starring at her bulging breasts.

Then another crewman from the boat stepped out and pocked a dart into one of her breasts. With a loud burst, a balloon popped, and we all doubled over and roared.

At daybreak we heard motors starting and by the time we got up nearly all the fishing boats were gone. Apparently the ocean wind had decreased, and the fishermen had gone back to work. Once more, we strolled the dock and once more the tranquility had returned. Gone was the party, the crowded dock, the action—and the tits.

Before leaving the cove however, we had one more thing to do. We couldn't leave without letting Herb try the springs. Now that I knew its location, we motored there and were able to hook the anchor well enough to leave the boat for a while. After rowing the dinghy into a slit in the rocks, the next swell threw us ashore in a semi-controlled crash and we leaped ashore, but the next swell drenched us.

After crash-landing the dinghy, we hauled it up, tied it to a rock, undressed and eased into a pool. A young couple, camping there, undressed and eased into the pool next to us. I tried not to stare at her and turned to Herb. He was trying to look at her face. In a few minutes however, we were all conversing as though the common nudity meant nothing.

Two little Indian kids who had come with family from the village, swam back and forth around our legs, laughing. A fisherman bathed with soap and washed his clothes in a small lower pool, exposed by the lower tide.

"Pool etiquette," he said. "Calls for soaping in the lowest pool."

Later however, a big black Labrador dog, with no etiquette, sprawled in the highest pool while we soaked below.

After dressing, we rowed back to *Fog Island*, hauled the anchor, and said a reluctant goodbye to Hot Springs.

Days later this drenching started rusting the knee joint in Herb's artificial leg and the lower leg wasn't swinging freely. So, he disassembled it, improvised a repair with engine tools, bronze wool and WD-40, and reassembled it. After strapping it back on he commented, "There's a little catch in one position, but it should work okay till we get home."

CHAPTER TEN

FINDING THE PERFECT BAY

Norm "Here's the next chart, Northwest Clayoquot Sound."

"I think that's pronounced, clackquit. Like the sound of that Herb?"

"Yeah. Who, other than a local, would know that?"

"I've been studying these charts for months. And this is one of my favorites."

"I see why. Look at all these neat little bays and inlets. Let's check out some of them. And what kind of an anchorage do we want for tonight?

"Well, it should have a good view of the sunset. And it should be naturally forested and maybe have some wildlife."

"And how about some crabs and oysters and maybe some bottom fish."

"And there should be no other boats."

"Definitely. We want it all to ourselves."

"First though, we've got to navigate past these submerged rocks off Sharp Point. Where do you think they are?"

"Imagine this, Herb. Imagine driving a car in an open prairie with no roads, where all you have is a map and some hills for landmarks. And suppose there are craters here and there and the craters are filled with dust, so that it all looks like solid ground. And if you happened upon one of the craters, you'd drive right off the edge. Isn't that like trying to navigate through these submerged rocks?"

I wished I had bought the detailed chart of this tricky area. On the chart we did have, I measured as accurately as I could, the distance from the point to the outer rock. Two tenths of a mile. And the inner rock was charted close to the point. To help locate them, we looked for waves breaking over either of the rocks. Nothing was breaking.

"If we stay about a tenth of a mile away from shore, we'll be halfway between the rocks. How many yards is that Herb?"

"There are about 6,000 feet to a nautical mile. So that's 600 feet, or 200 yards. Yeah, we ought'a be able to estimate that."

Herb slowed the motor, and I watched for the rocks from the bow. I looked in, out, and especially ahead. But we usually couldn't see underwater more than a boat-length or so because of surface reflections. And facing the sun as we were now, we couldn't even see that far. For a better view, I thought of chinning up the mast a ways as I'd done before. But with the boat's rolling, I was afraid to.

Here on the ocean, we also needed enough speed and power to turn through these waves in case we spotted a rock ahead. But at that speed if we didn't turn in time, an ocean wave could pound the boat into the rock and even crack the hull.

Herb was gradually and cautiously turning to round the point. That shifted the sun farther aft, and my underwater vision improved.

"Turn right! Quick!" I hollered.

Herb jerked the tiller aside and looked to see what I was trying to miss. "No. that's the shadow of the sail on the water."

"Damn! It's purple and even irregular in the waves like a rock would look."

"Yeah, scary."

After passing where we were pretty sure the rocks were and rounding the point, we turned acutely north into Sydney Inlet. We expected the prevailing northwest wind to then be against us—but it was the opposite.

"How about this wind, Herb. Can you figure it?"

"The ocean wind must turn and funnel into these channels. Let's not worry about it. Let's sail with it."

"Right! that's why we've got a sailboat."

There were other reasons for sailing. Tacit reasons. Because of our sick motor and to save gas.

We raised full sails, killed the noisy motor and rejoiced over the peaceful quietude. The only sounds were that of surf washing on the shore and of waves on *Fog Island*'s aft.

"Herb, just look at all this scenery. It goes on and on for miles. It's just too much. And there's nobody else here. This is why I wanted to sail around Vancouver Island. And it's worth it. Even with all the problems."

"Yeah, but too bad there aren't a few logging patches around."

I laughed. "You crazy Herb. Compare these green forests to those cleared swaths back in Quatsino Sound."

"Maybe I'm just prejudice because I used to be a logger."

It turned out that I wasn't alone in my thinking. In 1993, 18 years after our circumnavigation, some of the Tofino residents got tired of seeing the forests disappear, especially right across from them on Meares Island. "Keep Mears Green" signs were everywhere. They protested and even interfered with the logging operations. And they not only didn't stop protesting, but their group, Friends of Clayoquot Sound, got international attention. And that stopped the logging. Now, thanks to the protesters, Meares Island and its surroundings are still beautifully forested.

Ahead, inlets spread that were hard to identify. I walked forward, and holding the forestay, stood before the jib. "Captain

Vancouver, which inlet shall we take? In which bay shall we anchor? Ahoy, on the masthead. How far do the channels lead? Ready the longboats."

On the east side of the inlet, a small bay was charted behind a small island. Neither the bay nor the island were named. Although the bay's entrance was lined with rocks, a middle channel looked open. We couldn't resist. Herb turned the boat, the jib slapped over to the other side and I trimmed it. As *Fog Island* rolled into the bay's entrance, the waves dropped flat.

Two downed cedar snags lay the full width of a beach with their uplifted roots in the tree zone. From the middle of the two parent logs, forty-foot-tall children had grown. The children stood at angles from their inclined parents' bodies, as though straining for a closer look back at their parents' roots.

We anchored near a shoal connecting the small island to the main landmass and dinghied ashore. Herb tied the dinghy line around a big rock, between some oysters that were attached to it. He began picking the oysters, and with a big shell he found, dug some clams as well.

I walked the shoal and hiked across the small island. Usually, even in thick forests like this, there are old stumps, which are evidence of decades-old logging—but here there were none. This island had never been logged.

On the walk, my eyes were drawn upward by the untouched tall green spires. Others were silver-gray with their tops snapped off. Near the top of one of the tallest of these snags was an eagle's nest. Along the far shore, a moss devoured large portions of the living trees. Others lay jumbled on the beach. Climbing over, under, and around the logs, I made my way to a granite point and just sat there looking over Sydney Inlet and the ocean beyond—my form of meditation.

Several years before this, Canadian authorities trapped drug runners here in Sydney Inlet. The druggers had fled into one

Sydney Inlet

of the bays, ditched their boat and ran into the thick woods. Suppose they had pushed their boat off, leaving their departure point unknown. How would they have ever been found in this maze? Or, living off the land and sea, could some of them still be here?

Walking back to the boat, I couldn't find my original route. So, I worked my way right and left until I saw a beach. On it, there seemed to be the same logs I'd just seen on the last beach. Yes, it was the same beach I'd just left. Unknowingly, I had made a complete circle. When first crossing the island, I had apparently been more entranced with the trees than paying attention to where I was going. Finally, I was able to find my way back using an old reference—the sun. The shoal I'd crossed getting to the island was nearly covered by the rising tide so, now, I had to jump on its highest rocks to keep my feet dry.

By then, Herb had plenty of clams and oysters, so we set sail again, continuing to explore more of the inlet and running with the wind.

"Herb, let's go up the other side of the inlet. It looks like the mountains are lower there, and maybe I could get radio reception and call Mary Ann."

"Sure."

Once we reached the other side of the inlet, Herb began singing, "All day, all night, Mary Ann, down by the seaside siftin' sand."

"Alright, shut up. I'm going to call now."

"Tofino operator, Tofino operator. This is *Fog Island*, WYX 2946."

No answer.

Twenty minutes and a beer later, still no answer.

Running quietly and directly with the wind, we winged like a bird, with the jib billowing to one side and the main to the other. The sun set the small whitecaps aglow. For a better view ahead, I sat on the side of the cockpit, and from there, the dark blue water filling the deep V-shaped fiord was framed under the sails. Ducking my head to see behind the sails, tall cones and peaks seemed to puncture the sky. The shoreline ran as far as I could see as one continuous, narrow and perfectly uniform band. Using an endless chalk line, Poseidon must have trimmed the dense foliage to a precise horizontal line, cut exactly at the high tide line.

The last four-mile leg of Sydney Inlet seemed to transcend into a mountain lake, detached from the sea. Through the trees, we occasionally spotted small streams tumbling into the inlet. The wind softened, the boat slowed, but neither of us could reach for the starter button until the inlet's end.

The end of the inlet was a wide flat delta with scrubby vegetation—not a place we wanted to spend the night, so we turned around.

Returning, we were able to skirt the precipitous shoreline closely because the bottom dropped like an underwater cliff. In fact, we were so close to the shoreline that we had to watch more upward than sideways to be sure the mast spreader cleared the trees.

We turned a 180 in order to check out Holmes Inlet, and from there entered a nameless bay on the east side of the inlet through two constrictions narrow enough to spit ashore. Once in the center of the bay, we cut the motor and simply waited for *Fog Island* to stop its forward motion.

"It's totally silent, still. Let's call it 'Still Bay'."

"Cove sounds better than bay."

"Right. Let's sit and listen to Still Cove a few minutes."

Otters slithered along the shore, eagles soared, and a grouse drummed.

"This is nice, Norm. What do you think?"

"I don't see any oysters or clams and we only have enough for tonight."

"Okay," Herb chuckled. "It's still early. Let's do some more exploring. We can always come back."

Kind of shamefully, I pushed the starter button.

Just before the next tiny bay's entrance, we slowed the boat to watch some harbor seals playing near shore. As they dove, twisting and rolling against the shallow rock bottom, we eased toward them and they raised their puppy-dog heads, sometimes stretching them way above the surface to watch us with their big tranquil eyes.

The bay was barely large enough to anchor in. It was hemmed in and seemed to be claimed by the high surrounding mountains. We were used to more breathing room.

"Let's check Pretty Girl Cove, Norm. With a name like that, we've got to see it."

On the way there we noticed a narrow slit. "Are you thinking what I am, Norm?"

"It's a shortcut. But there won't be room to turn around once we're in it."

The chart showed no detail of the opening. It was too small. Herb slowed the boat to a crawl, and I watched from the bow. The shallow green rock bottom shelved way out from the right shore.

"Hard to port, Herb!"

His turn brought us almost onto the left shore.

"Damn, this is tight. I don't like it."

More rocks shelved out from the left shore.

"Hard starboard!"

That swing brought us almost onto the right shore again.

A red-breasted merganser with three babies scurried frantically out of our way and disappeared into a slot overlapped with trees.

When we started breathing again we spotted around the next point a high green knob above an immense lawn. Drawing closer, we saw that the lawn was actually the tidal grass of Pretty Girl Cove.

"Feels wide open doesn't it? The opposite from the last bay."

"I'll give you a bow watch again, Herb. How deep?"

"Eighty feet."

We continued into the cove.

"The bottom's coming up fast. Sixty. Faster now. Forty. Thirty."

"There's bottom! Right in front of us!"

We had two choices. We could either try to stop the boat or turn around. Even at our four-knot speed, reversing at even full throttle would have taken a good boat-length. That could have been too late.

Instead, the instant I hollered, "Bottom," Herb pushed the tiller hard to port. The boat turned quickly, but she pivoted such that her stern swung around in an outward arc. During its swing, the stern could have struck bottom. And I knew exactly what part of *Fog Island* would have hit bottom. I knew because I'd done it once before. And when I did, the boat could no longer be steered. The rudder had jammed against the hull.

We both stared at the clear green bottom moving toward the stern. We didn't speak. We waited to feel a crunch. We braced for it.

It didn't happen.

That turn took about five seconds—five of the longest seconds of the voyage. We figured that the rest of Pretty Girl Cove would be about the same, so under full sail, we departed.

Against the wind we tacked back and forth from one side of the inlet to the other, returning to the only other bay we hadn't checked—Young Bay. Entering the bay in the dying wind, we had to tack so close to the shore it scared some kingfishers from their perches. The water in the bay was fairly deep for anchoring, but near its head we found a 38-foot rise, so we dropped the hook and turned off the noisy motor.

"Wow Norm, look at this! It's got everything we asked for—a great view for the sunset, it's beautifully forested—and we've got it all to ourselves. And look at all those oysters over there."

"Let's see if it's got any bottom fish. Let's get in the dinghy and find out. How about trying at that kelp patch by the entrance."

From the dinghy, Herb lowered a bright metal jig to the bottom, reeled it in a little and began alternately jerking it up and letting it settle back down. He felt a sudden tug, then a jerking, and he reeled in and lifted a foot-long rockfish into the dinghy. He removed the hook, and after clubbing its spiny fat head with a stick, I lowered another jig. Got another one. In what seemed like no time at all, we had several fish slipping around our feet.

"Damn this is fun, Herb."

"It's great. I guess we'd better stop though. What are we going to do with any more fish?"

One by one, we laid the fish on a log ashore, drove an ice pick through its tail to hold it in place and with a sharp knife filleted the side of the fish against its backbone and ribs. After flipping each fish over and filleting its other side, we similarly peeled the skin from each of the fillets. That gave us a nice bag of meat which went on the ice in the boat's cooler. And using the fish carcasses for bait, we set the crab pot.

Then we rowed ashore to check out a ruins that were beside a deteriorated concrete foundation. Hundreds of worn bricks were strewn around. Just under the water some large metal pieces lay rusting.

Rowing back to the boat, we stopped by the oysters we'd seen entering the bay and dared ourselves. We each picked up a small one, opened it and slid the oyster into our stomachs.

A large lake, Lake Cecilia, was charted only a third of a mile beyond the inlet to the bay. I couldn't resist. Because the tide was fairly high, I was able to row the dinghy into the inlet and there, I tied it to a large branch ashore and found a trail, hoping it would lead to the lake. Rain forest trees roofed the trail and thick vegetation and windfalls surrounded it. The trail wove between the trees along the inlet stream and then rose, traversing a steep hillside above a box canyon. I climbed over and crawled under fallen trees, and on the steeper portions, hung onto the salal.

Fresh bear dung, full of berry seeds, lay piled here and there. Knowing I'd never be able to outrun a bear here, I whistled loudly.

Light appeared ahead, then an opening, then Cecilia Lake. I jumped from log to log on the drift jamming the lake's outlet. As I jumped, some of the logs rolled and a couple sank to my ankle before I could leap on to the next one. On some dry moss covering the top of a larger log, I sat and scanned the quiet pond. Movement on the water surface between the logs drew my eyes downward. Skippers. Smiling, I tried to catch one as I used to do for hours as a boy at our family's lake place.

A kingfisher chattered from a limb and took flight. It beat its way through the air, pulsating up and down, then tucked its wings and plunged, splash, catching a fish right in front of me. An eagle whistled. Then I headed back to the dinghy, and with two buckets of fresh water from the stream, rowed back to the boat.

"I think I've figured out those ruins, Norm. Listen to this in Nicholson's book. Why did the pilchards so mysteriously disappear? A two-million-a-year industry was wiped out overnight and both fishermen and biological experts are still seeking the answer. In 1925, the waters adjacent to the west coast of Vancouver Island appeared to be literally alive with them; large schools were frequently observed. By 1927, there were no less than twenty-six pilchard reduction plants between Barkley Sound and Kyuquot. The plants were together employing for a four-five-month season, 500 men ashore and another 500 represented in the various boat crews: 75 seine boats, 100 tugs and scouts, and 50 scows. Sets of 500 tons were occasionally made by one boat. Several other boats would go to her assistance, all sharing the fish. In 1946 not one showed up and there hasn't been a pilchard seen since!"

"Imagine that Herb—only forty years ago a busy plant was processing fish oil right over there at the ruins next to us. Anyway, why don't we contemplate that over a gin 'n tonic?"

"Good idea, Norm."

"I'm going to do it up right for a change and wash the salt out of our glasses with this pure Cecilia Creek water."

After sloshing out two glasses in the fresh water, I palmed some chipped ice from the cooler into the dripping glasses, filled them each a third full of gin and rationed in another third glass of our staling tonic. From a corner of the cooler, I dug out a piece of lime, squeezed it into the drinks and gave them a couple twirls with my finger.

"Here's to the departed pilchards. I think they got tired of seeing their buddies turned into oil, and they all swam away."

Herb had soaked the clams he'd dug earlier in saltwater to wash the sand out of them. Now he dumped them into a kettle on the stove burner. When the clams gave up and opened their shells, he passed them above along with some margarine he had melted. One-by-one we pried their hot shells apart and twisted out their meat with forks. We tossed the shells over our shoulders, dipped the clams into the margarine and slid them off the forks with our teeth. For a fingerbowl, we set a bucket of Young Bay seawater between us and found that from the protected bay, the water was actually warm.

I checked the crab pot in the dinghy. Two large ones. After throwing three smaller ones back, I grabbed the larger ones, carefully holding their pincers and legs to each side while they were struggling to pinch my fingers and cracked off their carapaces with a blow to the hard corner of the dinghy. Herb immersed the still-wiggling crab parts into boiling seawater, cooked them several minutes and dumped them in fresh seawater to cool. With loud cracks, we broke the toughest segments with our teeth.

"Better use our molars for this, doc."

"Ha. Yeah. We've improvised a lot of things on this boat, but even as dentists we'd have a heck of a time making a cap for one of our incisors."

"Norm, why don't you dig out some wine and I'll cook the oysters."

"I won't turn that down. But I think all we've got left is that old acid red stuff."

In the bottom edge of a compartment near the bilge, I dug through some soggy paper bags in a soggier cardboard box where we kept the wine to keep the bottles from breaking. Then, just when we needed it most, the damn corkscrew broke—but we found that a big screw in a vice grip worked just as well.

Herb poured the oysters into a pan lined with aluminum foil, added cut onions and some miscellaneous leftovers and several spices. Then he put the pan in the hot oven beside two potatoes, and the more of the wine we drank with the crab, the less acidic it tasted.

When it was cooked, I took a bite of the Herb special and exclaimed, "This is the best damn dinner I've ever eaten."

"Sure. And I suppose the best wine too."

After the big dinner I loosened my belt and there we sat, letting our stomachs digest the food and our livers detoxify the wine. There was a muffled drumming sound—a grouse. A great blue heron, looking like a pterodactyl, glided by. A large black-and-white mass fell to the water but stopped just before touching it. The yellow-beaked bald eagle rose, soared and dove again, both times unsuccessfully. An insane yelling startled us. Looking through binoculars, we spotted a loon, its throat pulsating. A speck on the water surface disappeared;

then reappeared—a pied-billed grebe. We heard a grinding sound ashore and looked in that direction.

A black stump ashore turned out to bear and it roamed the beach grinding on mussels with its teeth for about an hour.

Weakening spirals flitted back and forth across the bay. Each spiral of the hidden Swainson's thrushes ended in silence. Silence except for the sound of a gurgling stream.

"Hasn't Young Bay turned out to be everything we'd wanted. Look, here comes the sunset."

Like the "Canadian Sunset" I'd seen earlier in the trip, a tall picket fence began to grow along the eastern shoreline—an ever-changing fence of pale green trees illuminated by the setting sun. I turned my head to the west and watched the setting sun become red, and just before setting, I was able to peer directly into its heart, and in two minutes it was gone. I turned my head back and the fence was gone too. Above where the fence had stood, a ghost shadow rose, which gradually extinguished the trees as the sun set farther and the shadow climbed the hills and finally covered the highest mountains.

Lacy pink clouds barely moved. Suddenly, with a magic stoke, Venus cast them gray. And just as suddenly, displeased with her drab color choice, splashed pink back onto most of them. Soon she dashed them with dark ink and again, knowing she'd overdone the darkness, colored them all an eerie pinkish grey.

Beyond the clouds, the western sky was dark blue, then brilliant yellow, then pink. Silhouetted in the center of the blue, the yellow and the pink, a distant mountain remained constant.

The eastern sky was now black. Then the moon appeared like an immense flashlight, shining through the trees, and it rose, and kept rising.

The thrushes stopped singing. The mast and rigging stood motionless. There was no surf. No foghorns. Only the sound of the gurgling stream. Herb set his glass on the seat, and I jerked my head at the sound. Even my breathing was noisy. I breathed more softly.

The surface of the water was still. When either of us shifted our weight, the boat rolled slightly and started wavelets. I stopped shifting my weight.

Most of the shores grew black and indistinguishable. Except for the shore across from the moon which remained barely illuminated—a night-snow-gray.

I took my usual evening walk around the deck, hung the kerosene lantern in the rigging, tied an extra turn on the anchor line cleat, and before bed, stood there thinking, as Robert Service wrote, "It's the beauty that thrills me with wonder. It's the stillness that fills me with peace."

CHAPTER ELEVEN
TO TOWN

*A*s we were leaving Young Bay in the morning and looking at the chart, I said to Herb, "Well, now we've got plenty of time. It's only about 30 miles to Tofino and we've got three days to get there. Where do you want to go?"

"This inside route looks a little longer, but it keeps us off the ocean and there are some neat looking inlets along the way."

"Yeah, and here's a neat looking bay at the head of the first inlet. Bacchante Bay. It's about a mile long, but it's totally protected and in the pocket of some big mountains. It looks like it might turn out to be one of the best bays in the whole sound."

"And it's close. After all we've been through lately, we deserve an easy day for a change."

The bay was surrounded by steep heavily wooded hillsides. Beyond that a row of sharp peaks punctured the sky. We dropped the hook. With a nice long afternoon ahead of us, we rowed the dinghy up a stream at the head of the bay. It turned out to be so shallow that in places we had to drag it over the bottom, but it was worth the effort. Old-growth cedar forests stood right beside us. The base of some of the trees were about as wide as *Fog Island* was long. Several bald eagles flew by close and along the way we ate wild blueberries. One tree had much of its bark torn off and at a closer look there appeared to be bear claw marks all over it.

After dinner back at the boat Herb went below and read in his bunk. I sat above surveying our private bay. I talked with the crows and daydreamed over the chart.

In the morning we opted for a shorter but iffier route to Tofino. Sulphur Passage was narrow, rocky and two miles long, but we had done things like this before. With a bow watch, we slowly motored through the zigzag passage, and began to actually enjoy it.

Then we headed into narrow Matilda Inlet for a place charted as Ahousat with a store and fuel. It turned out to be nothing more than that. We had another reason for making this stop. After all the motor problems we'd been having, we were suspecting dirt in the fuel tank. We couldn't see into the tank even with a flashlight, so we dipped a stick into it, swirled it around, and it came up filthy. We knew we had to remove the tank and clean it thoroughly. After a couple hours of struggling, we got the tank onto the fuel dock, sloshed it around and dumped its contents into a bucket. We couldn't believe what flopped into the bucket. A large mushy mass of sawdust. The only way that could have gotten into the tank was to have been swept there, through the fill hole in the cockpit sole, probably during construction of the boat by a disgruntled workman. We finally knew what was causing all of our engine problems. The store owner, Hugh Clark, a stocky guy with no neck and no expression, showed us where to dump the bad fuel. We had met Hugh's brother, Jim, at Hot Springs. After dumping the bad fuel with its mushy contents, we sloshed out the tank repeatedly with fresh fuel, going back and forth between the dock and dumping it. While doing all this Hugh's little boy was watching us and telling us about cougars that had been killing their goats. Finally, we replaced the tank, filled it, cleaned the fuel line, fuel filter and carburetor and cleaned up the mess we'd made on the dock and in the boat. The motor started right up and ran perfectly.

After the trip, I talked to my boat dealer in Seattle about the sawdust in the tank. They contacted the Ranger boat company. They seemed to take no responsibility for the problem even though it was a new boat. I was furious, but the dealer said that it probably wouldn't be worth pursuing, so after sleeping on it a few nights, I gave it up.

Because there was no phone at Ahousat, we went farther into the inlet to the large Indian village of Marktosis, where there was supposed to be a phone. The houses there were all pretty weathered and the yards unkempt. Walking alone trying to find the phone, I felt uncomfortable with cold stares from the residents who apparently weren't used to seeing a white person in their village. While making my calls a playful little Indian kid squeezed into the broken-down phone booth with me. Even with the poor phone reception, Mary Ann and I were able to make plans for meeting after the boat trip. I was also able to reach my kids as well as their mother. Chris and Sheri said they'd just been playing outside and were looking forward to seeing me. Matt said he was playing on the floor with some toys. Their mother, Martha, and I had a short but good conversation. I hugged the Indian kid beside me and walked back to the boat, this time smiling back at all the stares.

"Herb, after all this time with the fuel tank mess, I say we find another close place to spend the night."

"I couldn't agree more. How about Whitepine Cove? It's right across the channel."

"You think we can get into this western part of it that's all by itself?"

"Let's see if we can squeeze through that narrow entrance."

The entrance was not only narrow and tortuous but shallow as well, so we slowed to a crawl, snuck between the rocks on both sides and took an immediate left to avoid hitting a shoreline that jumped out right in front of us. We dropped the

*Norm's three children, left to right,
Chris, Matt, and Sheri.*

hook in the most isolated part of the bay, had a well-deserved drink, enjoyed dinner, and watched the shoreline gradually darken with the setting sun.

With plenty of time remaining, we decided in the morning to check out Quait Bay on our way to Tofino. It looked isolated all by itself off to one side of our route and it turned out to be more beautiful than we had expected, so we dropped the hook for a while and listened to a gurgling stream right behind us. A kingfisher got caught in our rigging, chattered frantically, then freed itself and flew off. Later it splashed into the water beside the boat and came up with a fish in its beak. Showing off. Another one flew at the one with the fish and had a chattering fit, trying to get the fish, and then gave up. A red breasted merganser with seven young ones was preening on a nearby rock. Rhinoceros auklets, Storm petrels and little Cassin's auklets floated around here and there, and a bunch of gulls and Murres were hovering over herring balls.

"You know, Norm, this Clayoquot Sound is too much. I think these last three bays have been some of the best parts of the trip."

"Yeah. And isn't it something that they've been right in a row."

"And aren't we lucky we've had plenty of time here to enjoy them. But now we've got to break the spell and head for a town."

"I guess I'm ready for that."

In thick fog we then navigated the entire passage, buoy-to-buoy and island-to-island, as best we could by dead reckoning. After three hours, right in front of us bursting out of the fog, was a dock full of boats and several buildings. Tofino.

To celebrate we played pool in a pub with some of the locals. Showing off, I hit the cue ball low and hard, jumped it over one of their balls and hit and sunk one of our balls. How did these stiff-faced guys react? They didn't. For the first time since Herb came aboard, we then went to an actual restaurant for dinner and just sat there looking at each other like *What's this?*

Now, after having been jammed together on a little boat for three weeks, it was time for Herb to return home. These three weeks were about half of the circumnavigation, and counting all the inlets we explored, it was about 500 nautical miles, or two and a half times the length of Washington state. We had been through some extreme ups and downs. All the way from groping through ocean fog without a motor to finding quiet bays, soaking in a hot spring, and finding Indian skulls staring at us. As Herb boarded the floatplane in the morning, we waved a quiet goodbye to each other. Now I'd be alone for five days before my next crew would arrive—for the last leg of the voyage.

CHAPTER TWELVE

EXPLORING ALONE

Now that I was finally in a town with real telephones and maybe good reception, I headed right for the nearest phone booth. These were the days before cell phones, so I seemed to be keeping the phone company in business that summer, and each time I did find a land landline, I used it.

Mary Ann said that she had a ticket to fly back to meet me after the boat trip. We planned to start with another boat trip, but this time just to the nearby town of Poulsbo and just sit at the dock for a change.

I was also able to reach my kids, and considering the marriage split, I was terribly relieved to hear them still sounding okay. They would be returning to Seattle with their mother in a few weeks, and after all this time apart, I told them I couldn't wait to see them and give them giant hugs.

Then I told them about Mary Ann and about her being aboard the first part of the trip and that she would be returning after the trip. They asked if we were going to get married and I said maybe. I stressed that even if we did marry I would still be seeing them all the time. I told them that Mary Ann wanted very much to meet them and to sometime have them meet her three boys. Chris, the oldest at age 12, and the more quiet and thoughtful type, said she knew how badly her mother and I had been getting along, and that she would be glad to meet Mary Ann and her boys. Sheri, at age 10, and the more off-the-top type, said she wanted pictures of them all. Matt, five, just said, "OK daddy."

Then I called my next two crewmen, George, a longtime dentist friend and my brother Ralph, also a dentist. They were both set to meet me in Tofino in five days as planned.

After those phone calls I sat on a bench for a while, just thinking about how well things were going—and about now having nothing to do but explore more of Clayoquot Sound for five days—all by myself.

First the boat needed restocking. I shopped at the grocery store, drugstore, liquor store, and hardware store and packed all the stuff back to the boat in a backpack. The boat needed refueling—and that turned out to be a surprise. The current at the fuel dock was so strong that, going with it, I couldn't slow the boat enough to jump to the dock. Then, trying it against the current I had to use so much power that I was barely able to jump. After refueling and buying some cod jigs at the dock store, I returned the boat to the main dock, took a real shower ashore for a changed, and sat refreshed in the cockpit.

I even went to a restaurant for lunch. Outside of a restaurant I found an ornate handmade Indian sweater hanging on a post. I left it at the front desk and said that if it wasn't claimed by the time I next came to town, I wanted it. When I did return, the sweater was unclaimed, and I've been wearing it ever since.

Even though I now had the five days to explore Clayoquot Sound by myself, this would be the first time I'd be traveling alone that much—and the loneliness of that started to sink in. So, to divert my attention, I grabbed some charts and started planning destinations—and loneliness began to subside. During these five days alone, I noticed that my mind went from counting the number of days I had to be alone to those I'd get to be alone.

The Indian sweater I found

First I wanted to head north again, to see some of the places Herb and I had bypassed coming to Tofino—starting with Blunden Island. It was a small island right on the ocean with ragged, irregular borders. It had an inner bay that looked reasonably protected so I decided to give it a try.

First however, I had to get through the expansive sandbars just north of town. When Herb and I had come this way, it was so foggy we couldn't see how bad it was, but now, especially with the lower tide, the channel looked so narrow I didn't know how I'd be able to squeeze through. I slowed the boat and watched the sandbars passing by on both sides and barely below the surface. And at the narrowest possible place, a big fishing boat roared past me, and I literally held my breath.

After the sandbars, I continued north and as I got into more open water, an unusually low island appeared. Drawing closer, it turned out to be a huge flock of seagulls like I'd never seen before and as I passed by, they stayed put, paying no attention to me.

While underway I got into the business of preparing the boat for my solo cruising. I removed the life ring and the overboard pole which were not only in the way but would be useless if I fell overboard traveling alone. Instead, I strung a long line behind the dinghy with several big knots tied into it and with some attached floats. These would be my last resort to try to grab if I did fall overboard. I tightened the lifelines, and as things got rougher, harnessed myself into the boat so that it would be about impossible to fall overboard.

Soon enough Blunden Island came into view. I headed for the bay where I'd hoped to anchor, but it turned out to be so small that in order to get some protection from the ocean, I had to anchor as close in to the beach as I dared. Too close as it turned out.

For company that evening I turned on the VHF even though the reception was broken. One report was from a drunken sounding skipper whose boat was stuck on one of the sandbars I had passed earlier in the day. In the silence of the black night, some large bolts of lightning flashed, and later asleep below, I awoke to a loud crash and a flapping sound from the deck that jolted me out of bed. Going above with a flashlight I found bird feathers all over the deck. Apparently a gull had hit the boat's rigging and fell overboard. I just sat there for a while staring into the blackness. I realized how vulnerable I was here, alone in this isolated place, right beside the open ocean.

Early in the morning there was a loud twang on the anchor line. It was stretched so taut I thought it would snap in two. The boat seemed to be higher out of the water than usual, so I peeked over the side to see why, and my weight there caused the boat to fall onto its side with a crash that nearly threw me overboard. Sure enough, the boat was hard aground.

After determining that there was no hull damage I rowed ashore, and with an otter watching me, tied the dinghy to a big whale bone and walked the beach while watching the boat righting itself with the incoming tide, sometimes with loud thuds caused by the bigger waves. While walking, hundreds of shore birds flicked here-and-there to get out of my way while wisps of fog were flying by.

Once comfortable that the boat would be okay, I rowed the two-and-a-half miles around the island, staying well away from where the ocean swells were breaking on the rocky shoreline. I watched voids being sucked empty by the troughs of the swells that were then plunged full with each of their crests. At one rocky point I tried jigging and in just a few minutes caught a two-foot rockfish and an even bigger lingcod—way more than I needed—so I kept on rowing.

I looked off toward the hot springs—and started thinking about maybe one more soak. This route to the springs would be different than the one Herb and I had taken, so I'd get to see new things. Back at the boat I tuned the radio to channel 16: "All stations, all stations, all stations, this is Tofino Coast Guard radio, Tofino Coast Guard radio, Tofino Coast Guard radio, for the latest weather report, turn to channel 24." The report was okay, the fog wasn't bad, and the wind had lightened, so guess where I headed?

Going inside of Bartlett Island looked more scenic and it got me off the ocean for a while. But seeing a seagull, barely showing its white flapping wings through the fog ahead, should have been my warning. The fog thickened until even the islets charted right in front of the boat disappeared. I dodged the first one at the last instant, then dodged the other way for a rock. Finally, after seeing no more signs of rocks, my bulging eyes seemed to ease back into their sockets.

After another hour and a half of light-wind motor-sailing, I saw through the thinning fog, what looked like the entrance to Hot Springs Cove—which this time I knew better how to enter and how to find the dock. Being alone, I planned for just how I would dock, especially with no other boaters there to help. After what seemed like a perfect docking however, I was almost sorry there were no other boaters there to watch what I'd just done. Knowing the trail better now, I headed right for the springs, and soaked off and on until just before dark and finally returned to the boat. Peeing beside the dock in the darkness, the splashing caused a brilliant sparkling phosphorescence.

In the morning, I set the crab pot beside the boat and ate one for breakfast, which made my stomach smile. And using just enough fresh water for coffee, my stomach kept smiling. After washing the dishes and my face with saltwater, I burned my trash ashore, as was done there.

Before leaving, I couldn't resist exploring by dinghy, a tiny slit beside the cove's entrance. The slit was actually a shoal connecting tiny Mate Island to mainland Vancouver Island and it turned out to be so narrow that in places there wasn't even enough room to row. So, with one oar, I had to either paddle or push against the bottom. On the other side of the slit, there was the wide-open Pacific Ocean, with a million surface speckles flashing. I found a protected place to tie the dinghy and walked about a mile, mainly jumping on drift logs. Along the way I picked up some blue and green glass fishing floats that had floated all the way from Japan. It turned out to be one of the most rugged and scenic beaches I've ever walked.

Also, before leaving, I couldn't resist one other thing. Sharp Point looked like a good place for bottom fishing—and in no time, I had a rockfish and a lingcod. In fact, over the many years since then, I can't ever remember not catching fish here. And learning from that, we've caught bottom fish off many other rocky points along the coast. Once however, we went in too close. While fishing from the bow, I ended up looking straight down into a deep rocky hole. I hollered back to the cockpit for the crew to reverse hard, and I dropped the fishing pole and hung on.

On the return trip to Tofino, the fog lifted, and the waves were down, so I nosed into what's commonly called Cow Bay. Slowing way down, I watched several gray whales rolling gracefully, some only a few boat-lengths away. Then I needed to find tiny Tibbs Island which marks the channel to Tofino, but even with the binoculars, I couldn't find the light identifying the island until I was almost upon it. It turned out to be hidden on a side of the island rather than facing out to sea as would be expected. At the Garrad Group I steered very carefully because the island group turned out to be nothing more than a bunch of rocky reefs—which were suddenly all around me.

A bay just ahead had an inviting name. Whitesand Cove. Though it was fairly exposed to the ocean, the weather was good, and the report was for only 5 to 15-knot variable winds, so I decided to give it a try. However, because the whole cove was so shallow the only place I could find deep enough to anchor was charted at only one fathom. The boat would therefore barely clear the bottom on the night's low tide, but I figured at worst I'd only be grounded for a few hours.

Being this close to the ocean, ashore I tied the dinghy line tightly around a log with a clove hitch and three half hitches. On my beach walk, tiny sandpipers were scurrying everywhere along the high tide line, so I tried to keep out of their way.

Back at the boat I cooked the rockfish I'd caught earlier and while eating it for dinner, I had a kind of selfish feeling, with no one else there to watch the setting sun cast eerie moving lights along the entire beach. With the incoming tide in the morning, I watched the sky lighten over the Catface Range with ever-changing colors of pastel orange, yellow, amber, and then blue. The sounder read six feet. That gave the boat about one foot of clearance, so I just sat and watched more of the sunrise.

My thoughts drifted back to the burnout. I thought again about how I might approach dentistry more like a craftsman. I had always enjoyed woodcrafts, so wouldn't I like that approach better—trying to shape each filling like carving a piece of wood—perhaps to even greater detail than I'd done before. Psychologists say the key to enjoying one's work is an old, nearly forgotten principle: do your best. Not just for the patient's sake, but for my own.

I'm afraid that over the years I've observed that average American dentistry isn't really very good. This first struck me when I was stationed at West Point in the Army, where I spent half of my time replacing relatively new, but failing fillings on these young cadets, who were some of our most fortunate young citizens from all parts of the country, and who should have exhibited the best of dental care.

Another thought came to mind. How lucky I was to be a dentist. We dentists have skills no other professionals have. We can cut dense calcifications in sharp detail and restore them to last years—and we can do all that through an opening the size of a knothole. This should be something worth remembering the next time I get stressed.

After passing Tofino, I headed for the innermost portion of Clayoquot Sound, Tofino Inlet. This would be the last part of my exploration alone and the part I'd been most looking forward to. The inlet had so many neat channels and bays I didn't know where to start. On the way there, little Gunner Inlet looked too good to pass up. It had a small inner bay that looked just right for solitude.

Something else grabbed my attention. A huge horseshoe-shaped Kennedy Lake lay right beside the main inlet. In fact, it was even bigger than the entire inlet. It was connected to the inlet by what was charted as a river, but which was so narrow I questioned whether the boat could squeeze through. I had to find out when I got there.

The most direct route to the inlet was by way of Browning Passage. What I didn't realize was that this passage is considered unapproved, and I found out why. There were two large rocks charted right in the middle of the passage. I crept through what looked like a slit between them, barely making it. Then there were islets and sandbars everywhere. It looked like there was one windy slit between them all, so after watching the islands and sandbars slowly pass by on both sides of the boat, things finally opened up.

After all that, I dropped the hook in the first bay I could find. It was so silent there all I could hear was a low ringing in my ears and later, the sound of my teeth chewing dinner. Five "cruisers" floating by the bay's entrance turned out to be loons, and to prove it, they yodeled loudly. The snags ashore appeared as spires against the darkening sky and after listening to the owls hooting for hours I crawled into my bunk.

The morning cloud formations were ever-changing. Directly above was a pattern of thin cirrostratus clouds and inland from that were two zones of striated clouds crossing each other obliquely and above all that, some thick morphing loops, bows and hooks that looked like cotton that a child was playing with, pulling it here and there. My sunglasses were scratched, bent and stepped on, so I washed them for a change and the clouds looked even better.

Kennedy Lake was now close enough to give it a try. But I couldn't get into it. Even by dinghy, the lake's outlet stream narrowed so much that I was actually blocked by a large group of angry mergansers frantically thrashing at me.

So instead, I sailed quietly into nearby Tranquil Inlet. Near its end I entered a tiny bay so stunning that before anchoring I cut the motor just to hear, see, and feel it better. At the head of the inlet, I took a long soak in a tide pool while watching an otter family climbing back and forth over some piles of drift.

Seeing no other boats in Tofino Inlet, I seemed to have the entire inlet to myself—just me and the otters.

For spending the night, Gunner Inlet turned out to be just right. By evening wolves were howling with undulations that sounded like sirens. The moon refused to show its face to the few stars, and the sky cast an inky gray reflection in the water with little junction between the land and sky and no junction at all between the land and the water.

My mind drifted to the kids. They were playing there in the cockpit, with Chris and Sheri on both sides of little Matt, playfully tormenting him. Then my mind shifted to Mary Ann. She was sitting there beside me, smiling.

Being alone now, my mind then shifted back to the burnout. Something new came to mind. How about trying to limit my feeling of responsibility. I thought about how much of the population smokes knowing it may kill them. So why should they floss their teeth. We obsessive-compulsive dentists—the personality type attracted to dentistry—tend to think that our work should be perfect and never fail—one reason for the profession's high suicide rate. Physicians seem to feel less responsible for the loss of a life than we for the loss of a tooth. Something to think about.

Another thing came to mind. How about trying to listen better to a patient's underlying considerations about his teeth. Does he care more about their appearance, function, and longevity, or is it about his time money, or fear of pain. And then, addressing his primary concerns in an objective way, I could present a treatment plan that he'd be more likely to accept. And that should not only help me enjoy my job more and ease the stress.

Walking ashore in the morning, I noticed a large dog coming my way. When it neared, I saw that it was actually a wolf. I scurried back to the dinghy and readied an oar for clubbing him. But he just kept walking along the beach, paying no attention to me, so I sat there for a while and watched him.

Back at the boat I put on the cleanest and driest of my clothes and after listening to some distant thunder and waiting for the weather to clear, I headed back to Tofino.

How many times have I been to Tofino since then? Too many to remember. Over the years it has become kind of a second home. I've gotten to know some of the locals well enough that they've invited me to their homes.

One problem with Tofino, even in the summer, is the rain. The average annual rainfall is about 300 inches and during one recent June, it rained every single day. On the other hand, the summer rains aren't usually very bad—or was I just getting used to them?

How about the wind? Usually about right for sailing. But not in August 1991. I was in my 37-foot sailboat, docked along with some other boats at the crab dock and we were getting hammered by a surging chop. It rained in blasting horizontal streaks and five inches were reported overnight. When I peeked out of the hatchway, blinding wind and water tore across my face. Storm warnings were upgraded to hurricane warnings— that's 75 miles per hour and in some parts of town it was blowing even harder. Our boats were bouncing like corks, and the wharf, like another cork. To avoid snapping the mooring lines, I tied the boat so loosely I couldn't jump to the dock and even then two of my many lines snapped taut and broke with a loud frightening blast. The deck of a powerboat next to me was torn from its hull, another powerboat was awash, and a metal skiff sunk. One of the main dock pilings broke loose, and the dock started to come apart. I was worried, but there was nothing I could do but wait it out. By morning the wind was down, and I could see that some of my mooring lines had come loose, some had worn over halfway through at the chocks and most of them had worn deep grooves in the four-by-four dock railings.

Nothing like outlasting such a fierce storm to make a person feel fully alive. In fact, over the years I've even gotten to the point where things like this that used to scare me, now just keep me alert.

Just three weeks after that, there was yet another hurricane. This time however, I was anchored in a bay farther from the ocean—but still, I didn't know what would happen. I let out more anchor line, backed off on it at full power and hoped for the best. Some of the trees were blowing nearly sideways and the downpour created several streams I'd never seen here before, and the streams were all gushing into the bay with heavy layers of foam and brackish water. The swirling water was twisting the boat back and forth so violently I couldn't stand up without hanging on with both hands.

So why do I keep going back to this crazy place? Have you ever sat anchored in a bay with nothing but you and the ducks, and watched the setting sun turn the sky a brilliant red, and then watched the rising moon set the distant mountains aglow, while the stars tumbled out—and wondered if you were dreaming?

CHAPTER THIRTEEN
A SEA OF ISLANDS

George and my brother Ralph came aboard in Tofino. We hesitated in leaving, not only because of the weather, but because the entire fishing fleet was still at the dock. We learned later however that they were not staying in because of the weather, but because they had already had such a good fishing season they didn't need to make more money and pay more taxes.

While we were waiting at the dock, the three of us looked over the chart of our next destination. Barkley Sound, the largest and most popular of Vancouver Island's west coast sounds, is a 17 by 17-mile sea of small islands. About two hundred of them, all heavily forested and uninhabited—and just right for exploring and secluded anchoring. We agreed to take our time here and to start by exploring what looked like the best part of the sound—the Broken Group.

"Look at Effingham Bay here," Ralph said. "It's wide open."

"And should be a great place to anchor," George said.

"I agree," I answered. And looking closer at the chart, I said, "Guess what's charted right across the isthmus of the Island? It says right here in small print, 'Indian Village'."

"Wow, what more can we ask for?" Ralph said. "A wide-open bay and some really neat exploring."

"Okay," I answered. "Let's definitely spend a night there."

"Here's another place," George said. "Look at Wouwer Island. It's right on the ocean."

"Finding a protected place to anchor this close to the ocean looks iffy." I said. "But if we can anchor is this little inside bay, it looks okay, and it's only a short walk across the island for a perfect ocean view."

Sailing for Barkley Sound the next day, we turned in close to the shoreline at five-mile-long Long Beach—the longest sand beach on the Canadian coast. We slowed down and watched several gray whales rolling and about 70 sea lions roaring loudly on a small rock island.

The fog thickened at the worst possible time, just as we were entering the sound. We lowered the sails, motored slowly and had no choice but to creep between the sound of big ocean waves crashing on the shore just to our left and other barely visible waves breaking over the ugly green reefs to our right. The farther we got away from the ocean the more the fog lightened. Then there it was, right in front of us, Barkley Sound, with dozens of its wooded islands now visible.

The first thing we did was to stop at Ucluelet for fuel. The dock attendant welcomed us with this: "Welcome to Barkley Sound. It's a sea of rocks and they're shaped like pyramids and only a fourth of them are charted."

Once in the tightly compacted islands of the Broken Group, we slowed down, often with a bow watch. Even doing that however, we found one of those rocks the dock attendant had warned us about. What a scare, hitting a rock that seemed to come up from out of nowhere, but it seemed to have caused no damage, so we kept going.

After anchoring in a niche in one of the islands, we spotted what looked like abalone on the bottom. I put on my wetsuit, weighted waist belt, fins, and mask. While holding my breath, I dove, and one-at-a-time, pried several of them off the rocks with a screwdriver. We pounded them with a hammer, breaded and fried them—one of the best lunches I'd had on the trip.

Does this mean I had diving experience? No. Before the trip I'd bought the wetsuit just in case it was needed to check the bottom or to try to make an underwater repair. Otherwise, we would have had to find a place where we could beach the boat and wait till low tide to get to the bottom.

It turned out that we needed the wet suit for something else. While stopping at an abandoned houseboat, the prop tangled in one of its sunken lines and the motor stopped. We couldn't turn the shaft from inside the boat even with wrenches, so I dove and was able to free the prop.

While traveling through the islands, we passed some deep caves. We anchored and walked into one of them and found what looked like finger bones. Knowing that the Indians buried their dead in these caves, we left the bones untouched, and we didn't stay in the cave long for fear of the rising tide trapping us there.

As planned, we anchored for a night in Effingham Bay. Ashore, we walked across the isthmus and sure enough, there it was, just as charted—the ancient Indian village site. In a flat plateau there we found a 300- foot-long midden and near that, several nurse logs with hemlocks growing from them— but instead of being round, these nurse logs were squared, identifying them as the remains of what were the beams of four longhouses. There we stood, like being alongside some of the 10,000 original inhabitants of Barkley Sound eating shellfish beside their fires.

Relaxed that evening, I felt the need to bring up my stress with dentistry. Their response surprised me.

George, being basically a happy-go-lucky extrovert, seemed to get over any stressors quickly and just go on with filling the teeth. He started his practice well after mine, and he came by my office for advice about how to run the business. Dentists, especially back then, didn't learn much about the business side of dental practice. He appreciated my advice and we've stayed good friends ever since.

Ralph was also easygoing. In fact, even as a children's dentist who deals with lots of unruly kids, he doesn't seem to get ruffled. I've watched him hold a squirming kid's head back in the dental chair while calmly treating a tooth and talking with me about something else. I asked him how he can handle this, and he says he doesn't pay attention to it, and like George, just goes on with filling their teeth. I thought that if he could do this with squirming kids, why shouldn't I be able to handle well-behaved adults? This would be something to think about the next time I get stressed—and try to be more like my own brother.

After cruising through some of the other islands, we headed for our next planned destination—Wouwer Island. We worked our way into what looked like the one possible anchorage, so

Ocean side of Wouwer Island

we dropped the hook. On our way ashore in the dinghy, we checked out a small rock island with dozens of barking sea lions on it. We apparently approached too close because several of these thousand-pound sea lions jumped in the water, circled the dinghy, and while raising their heads out of the water right beside us, angrily showed their teeth. We had invaded their territory, and we didn't know what they would do next. We sat, motionless and breathless. Then, very cautiously, we eased away from them.

Ashore after that, we found a 40-foot gray whale lying on the beach, but still twitching. I kicked it to see if there was any hope but there was no response. When I was there the following year, there were just bones and I reached down, touched its big skull and said, "Goodbye."

After searching ashore, we found what looked like the vestige of a trail that seemed to cross to the ocean side of the island. It turned out to be nothing more than a salal tunnel that we had to crawl through—but it was worth it. The upper part

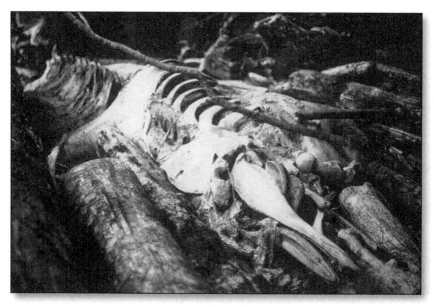

Whale bones

of the beach was choked like Tinkertoys with weather-beaten drift logs from probably hundreds of years of Pacific storms. After climbing over the logs and scaling some headlands, we walked the clear sand beach below, where there were several interconnected tide pools with streams all meandering down the beach. Everything was teaming with marine life, including carpets of mussels so tightly compacted that even a waxed thread couldn't have been flossed between them. Just ahead sea lions were roaring along the shoreline, and eagles were perched in shreds of storm-torn trees.

On future trips here I've told my crewmates beforehand that I was going to show them the most beautiful island in the world. And after seeing some of these things they would usually start agreeing with me.

Leaving Wouwer Island in the morning, we took a daring shortcut, trying to squeeze through a tiny slit to our west. It narrowed to only a couple boat-lengths in width, so without enough room to turn around, we crept through, watching the rocks passing under the bottom, hoping we wouldn't hear a crunch. It turned out to be the worst slit I've ever been through and a place where a bow watch would only scare you.

We couldn't believe what we saw next. As we started to round Austin Island, right in front of us was the bow of a ship protruding from the water. We learned later that it was the 10,500-ton freighter, *Vanlene* which ran aground here just a few years before. We couldn't

Shipwreck

resist approaching, wondering if there just might be anything to salvage, but in the ocean waves we weren't able to get close enough to find out.

Before the next day's long journey down Strait of Juan de Fuca we made a short stop at the small town of Bamfield to top off the fuel tank. Right beside the town's entrance channel cowered some large old buildings that looked very much out-of-place. They were the remains of the terminus of the 4,000-mile cable crossing from Australia, where at the turn of the prior century, part of the first round-the-world telegraph message was transmitted.

Because of the long trip down the strait the next day, we wanted to anchor as close to Cape Beale as possible. The only protected place we found was a tiny bight that was so choked with kelp it clogged the boat's water intake and overheated and stopped the motor. While the boat was drifting we detached the water intake line, cleaned out the seaweed clogging it, and once we got the motor running again we quickly anchored to avoid clogging the intake again. And there we sat watching the fog pour in relentlessly from the ocean.

With some extra time before dinner, we decided to row the dinghy ashore and have a hatchet throwing contest, like Ralph and I use to do while growing up in a woodsy area near our home. We took turns throwing the hatchet into the end of a drift log. I won the contest, but I had cheated. I'd been practicing along the way.

Tomorrow we would head for home, for the final leg of a remarkable one-and-a-half-month voyage. But first we faced the longest stretch of open water and perhaps the roughest part of the whole trip.

CHAPTER FOURTEEN
LONG SAIL HOME

On July 25, 1975, 0600 hours, departed Barkley Sound, in thick fog, headed for our Seattle home, on the last leg of the Vancouver Island circumnavigation. This is how the day's log began.

It was a remarkable voyage—but now I was ready to go home. I would soon be cleaning up, and for the first time in over six weeks, shaving and using deodorant. Then I would be reunited with my three precious kids. And later meeting with a beautiful Mary Ann.

Now we faced the full length of the nearly 100-mile-long Juan de Fuca Strait. This would not only be the longest stretch of open water of the voyage, but it could also be the roughest part, because when the typical westerly winds meet the ebbing current here, it builds up a chop that's often so bad it's considered unsafe for small craft. We would therefore have to plan our traveling around these long hours of adverse conditions. At other times however, we would be able to catch an optimum combination of the flooding currents along with these westerlies, which would drive us down the strait at record speeds. Luckily, this was the best time of the month for these favorable currents to be happening during our afternoon sailings. Besides wind and current there would be another problem, riptides, which I knew all too well from the horrible encounter we had with one here on the first leg of the trip. Because of these uncertainties, we were not able to plan ahead for where we might be stopping or spending the nights.

Norm and Ray Williams, years later

In the morning's thick fog, we hauled anchor and headed for home. We rounded invisible Cape Beale, listening to its foghorn blaring beside us. Thousands of murres and shearwaters scooted out of our way, right in front of the boat. Through the sometimes-lifting fog, we began to see miles of tilted, multicolored sandstone shelves as well as caves, arches, blowholes, and beaches notched between bulging headlands. It was like Vancouver Island was giving us a last beautiful goodbye.

We spotted what looked like the entrance to Nitnat Lake. It was very narrow, and we'd read that there was a sandbar there that could be dangerous to cross. However, we couldn't help but wonder what it would be like.

Years later I found out.

With some extra time here and fairly calm weather, we decided to give it a try. The entrance looked too tight to enter so we anchored just outside, and with some gray whales rolling beside us, proceeded by dinghy. After passing through the rollers over the bar and dodging the rocks in the narrow channel, the long lake opened up in front of us. Compared to the gray rolling ocean we'd been in all this time, the lake was a deep blue color, the surface serene, and it was surrounded by long sandy beaches. A man from a reserve there came out in a small boat to greet us, and he introduced us to a merganser duck he had aboard named Sawbill. We stopped at a beach, but only for a short time before heading back to the boat, because we were afraid of any weather change trapping us there.

Several miles past Nitnat Lake, we passed a gushing waterfall. Tsusiat Falls poured over an 80-foot cliff directly onto an ocean beach. Along the way here we saw people hiking the 47-mile West Coast Trail between Bamfield and Port Renfrew. The trail was constructed in 1907, after the 126 survivors from the shipwrecked Valentia were unable to make it out by foot because of the impenetrable underbrush.

Does the fog usually lift like this so you can see things along the way? Nope. Once here we were in fog all day long, starting in the ocean and down the full length of Juan de Fuca Strait, all day straining our eyes to see something—anything. That was one of the longest days of my life. And that's why I call the island Fog Island.

After a few hours of sailing, the westerlies began to pick up, and together with a flooding current, the land was whizzing by at twice the normal speed, especially when surfing down the front sides of the bigger waves.

The fog socked in again. Unable to see land for hours, we followed the 15 to 25-fathom curve down the coast, which we figured would position us in the only safe zone—less than a mile from the hazardous shoreline yet inside the freighter traffic.

Brothers return

After groping for it in the fog, we found the entrance buoy to Port San Juan, and holding our breaths, we turned straight into what would otherwise have been the side of Vancouver Island. Twenty minutes later, no land in sight, only the thick fog. The sounder read nine fathoms, the swells were down, and we hadn't hit land yet, so we assumed we were in the harbor. The three of us were all eyes, alert and wondering. Suddenly, a glow appeared from above. It grew into a yellow shaft of light, and it streamed right down unto the town of Port Renfrew. We looked in awe, as if the heavens had opened up to help us navigate. Within seconds the fog ahead disappeared, the sun became bright, and the sky was as beautiful a blue as you'd ever hope to see. We had ended up right where our navigation told us we should be, in the center of the harbor. We docked at Port Renfrew, and after rounding up someone to pump some gas for us, we celebrated by spending much of the night in the pub with the locals.

As we were departing in the morning, Ralph spoke up. "Norman, I've been thinking about your burnout problems, and I've come up with something that should help—a lot. Why don't you have a new office built. For the last ten years you've been in that old, cramped rented office. It even leaks sometimes. Isn't that true? How about a brand-new office about twice that size? You definitely need more space. Wouldn't that be nice—and wouldn't that decrease your stress a lot? In fact, Norman, I've been thinking about moving too. How about a new office building for the two of us?"

"Wow Ralph, what a great idea."

"Thanks."

"But are you sure you can stand working that close to your mean old brother?"

"Another thing, Norman. You might want to stop taking in all those associates. They cause too much stress. Back off and simplify."

For years I'd had two associates, working in the office in overlapping shifts. It was like a zoo. The longer they were there the more they wanted, and what they wanted was mine. Complications continually arose, and after a day of arguing about who would use which dental chair and when, who would get the room with the electrosurgery or the one with the nitrous oxide, why instrument trays weren't ready right when they wanted them and why I wouldn't lower their rent, I came home exhausted and exploded over a double Jack Daniels.

"You're absolutely right Ralph. This is something I've been thinking about too. So, when the next associate leaves, I'll think twice before replacing him."

We sailed down the rest of the strait in increasing westerlies, still surfing down the big waves at twice the usual speed and with the whisker pole bowing out under the pressure of the billowing jib. Suddenly it felt like the boat put on its brakes. I looked back and saw what we should have predicted—the towed dinghy was under water and dragging like an anchor. Because of the roughness we weren't able to get it aboard or retrieve it, so we had what seemed like little choice but to let it go. Hours later, the radio reported a boat finding a lost white dinghy with a blue stripe. Ours. Later in Seattle it was returned, and I gave the finder a big tip.

Back in fog, we groped into Port Angeles. Without a chart of it we landed at the first dock we could find and there, we cleared Customs.

In the morning, 20 to 30-knot west winds were predicted. Because that would be against a full ebb current, we stayed put for a while. As we departed a few hours later there were four loud whistle blasts, and out of the fog a Coast Guard boat appeared that was towing a broken-down fishing boat. We jerked out of its way, and before long, we heard an even louder but more distant whistle, this one apparently from the Coho ferry coming from Victoria. We honked back repeatedly, hoping she would see us on her radar. Finally, the sound of the whistle got weaker and we relaxed.

George kept asking about using the stove, which we rarely used underway. I was reluctant, but when the waves decreased some, he lit the burner, closed the hatch, opened some cabin windows and Ralph and I wondered what he was doing. An hour later he appeared with non-other-than a fresh strawberry shortcake. Ralph and I couldn't believe our eyes. George had secretly bought the ingredients while we were in Port Angeles. This was his celebration of a great trip, now coming to completion.

At the beginning of the trip we had practiced using the RDF in this area. Now in the fog, it was for real. We zeroed in on Dungeness, Race Rocks, and Point Wilson. As the fog lifted, there it was straight ahead, Point Wilson, just as the RDF showed.

After rounding the point, we checked the chart for a place to anchor for the night. Straight ahead was a narrow canal with a bridge over it. It would be the first bridge of the voyage. Although the bridge was charted at well above our mast height, I'd always tensed the instant the mast comes under a bridge. There was a reason for this apprehension. When learning boating years before, I once made a terrible mistake. I hit the Fremont Bridge in Seattle. There was a loud crash, and the impact snapped the forestay, leaving the mast to bash into each girder of the bridge. I watched, petrified.

Just past the bridge we anchored in Oak Bay, finally back in the protected waters of our Puget Sound home. To celebrate our last night aboard we played poker well into the night. But after the long day of navigating through fog, we were tired—until George suggested removing the betting limit. After placing a $100 bet, I did my best to keep a poker face while holding two wild cards that made a straight flush. Ralph dropped out. George called me and I got worried. He felt pretty sure of himself with his straight flush, but unlucky for him, mine was higher. A fitting reward for my completion of a wild but wonderful circumnavigation.

Anxious to get home, I hauled anchor early in the morning while Ralph and George slept. I set both sails and quietly headed south in light but increasing north wind. A strange buzzing sound startled me. It kept repeating. Off the bow a gigantic gray whale rose. I froze. But no, I realized that the gray was metal. What? A submarine! It dove and then resurfaced, all the time buzzing. Finally, after both the sub and the buzzing disappeared, I relaxed, with the wind now carrying us home.

It was time to make some final plans about my burnout. I lashed the tiller and made a list. And rather than slipping back into my same old habits, I vowed to make these changes as soon as I returned.

1. Remember how lucky I am to be a dentist.
2. Approach dentistry like a woodcraft.
3. Cut stress
4. Stick with the teeth rather than office business.
5. Stay on schedule without feeling rushed.
6. Improve staff performance
7. Improve or eliminate disagreeable patients
8. Limit my responsibility
9. Build a better office

My mind shifted back to some of the voyage's more intractable problems. Like how many times the motor had broken down—forcing us to sail into ports we'd never seen before. Yet being thankful we had a sailboat. So that when that mysterious hunk of metal goes cold, and after glaring at it and attacking it unsuccessfully with tools, I could go above, set the sails—and have that pull of the wind ease my frown. In fact, I've learned from this that when things go wrong in general, there's always a brighter side and that can ease a frown.

Then my mind shifted to the best parts of the voyage. Like soaking in the hot springs with my arms gurgling. Like the skulls staring back at us in the Indian burial ground. Like those quiet bays, with nothing but the ducks, and watching the setting sun turn the sky a brilliant red, and watching the rising moon set the distant mountains aflame, while the stars tumbled out.

In the serenity of bays like this, the headaches of the voyage seemed to disappear and then…the inevitable—I started thinking about another circumnavigation.

AFTERWORD

What happened with Mary Ann? We married and moved to a beautiful woodsy property with her three boys. We continued Vancouver Island boating as well as two extended voyages to the Bahamas, one with her kids and one with mine. After many wonderful years together, problems developed and we separated, however we have remained close ever since, and her boys and I have continued taking many boating trips together.

What happened with my burnout? The voyage not only distracted me from that, but I learned much from my crewmates—like how to stick with the teeth rather than the office business and moving to a better office. One of the first things I did after returning from the voyage was to have a new office built. After ten years of renting an old, cramped office, I moved into a modern office twice that size. That tripled the growth of the business, yet surprisingly, at the end of each day I felt less tired.

Taking the voyage also turned out to be one of the best things I've ever done for my life.

ABOUT THE AUTHOR

Norm Culver started boating at age three in a leaky rowboat and 80 years later he was still boating. He has taken 22 major Vancouver Island voyages including nine circumnavigations of the island. These voyages were completed on five different sailboats, with crews of over one hundred. Altogether he has covered about 50,000 nautical miles, or over twice the distance around the globe.

Norm practiced dentistry in Renton, Washington for 33 years and following that, conducted dental seminars internationally for 20 years.

He has written 26 boating and dental articles, one of which won a national prize. He has also written portions of the Waggoner Cruising Guide and Northwest Boat Travel.

Even though Norm has also skied and backpacked most of his life, his heart still strays back to those quiet anchorages with nothing but the ducks for company—and well, maybe a glass of wine.